FATHER BAKER

FATHER BAKER

Father Baker

by *FLOYD ANDERSON*

The Bruce Publishing Company   Milwaukee

NIHIL OBSTAT:

JOHN F. MURPHY, S.T.D.
Censor librorum

IMPRIMATUR:

✠ WILLIAM E. COUSINS
Archbishop of Milwaukee
May 4, 1960

Library of Congress Catalog Card Number: 60–13938

for
**OUR LADY
OF VICTORY**

ACKNOWLEDGMENT

IT IS impossible to name all those who opened their minds and hearts when asked for information about Father Baker, and whose retentive memories have supplied so much material for this book. However, a special debt of gratitude is owed to Monsignor Joseph M. McPherson, general superintendent of Our Lady of Victory Homes of Charity, without whose co-operation, guidance, and assistance this book would not have been possible.

FOREWORD

GOD gives to every man the personal mission of saving his immortal soul. This of necessity includes an influence for good on those with whom he comes in contact. To some few in each age and generation God gives a special added mission, something out of the ordinary to be done so that His divine purpose may be advanced. We who knew Father Baker are convinced that he was one of "the chosen few" who successfully accomplished a special and extraordinary purpose for which God sent him among us.

This book was written to acquaint you with this priest and his mission. A better understanding of both will come to those who follow the story of his life which Floyd Anderson has condensed in this book. We who assist in continuing his work are convinced that you will benefit by knowing more about our beloved "Father Baker"; that knowing him better you will come closer to his (and our) beloved "Our Lady of Victory." Of course, everyone who draws closer to our Lady inevitably comes in closer contact with her divine Son.

This in essence is why we hope as many as possible will read and enjoy this story of the life of Father Baker. Mr. Anderson makes no pretense at a definitive biography. We know that he has spent many hours and days at research and interview tracking down legends and stories about this great man. From that material he has developed this singular story of a simple priest who accomplished a gigantic task of service to humanity. As you will discover, this task was by no means simple except in its approach to the individuals he served.

Often we are asked, "Will Father Baker be canonized some day?" This is a question which no man can answer. We even hesitate to say, "We hope so." Whether it is in God's plan that Nelson Baker continue his mission by being officially declared a Saint by the solemn authority of the Church is hidden now as are many of God's intentions. It is certain, however, that Father Baker left us a heritage by which his special mission continues. As witness we have the institutions he founded and developed. Most of all we have the widespread devotion to Our Lady of Victory.

If, as we sincerely trust, this book brings you a greater concern for the needs of your neighbor, if it makes you love and depend on our Blessed Mother more and more in helping him, then indeed the story of Father Baker has been worth telling.

JOSEPH M. McPHERSON

FATHER BAKER

CHAPTER I

"BISHOP, the work on the national shrine to Our Lady of Victory is finished," said Father Baker happily. "We can now set the date for its consecration. Would May 25 be convenient for you?"

Bishop Turner frowned as he looked at the 84-year-old priest sitting in his office. "Consecration, Father Baker? You know the entire building must be completely paid for before it can be consecrated. You must be joking, Father."

Father Baker smiled. "Oh, no, Bishop. The national shrine is completely paid for — every last cent of it."

Bishop Turner shook his head. "I don't see how you did it, Father. The shrine cost over two million dollars — and it is all paid for? Why, that's a tremendous achievement. I heartily congratulate you, Father Baker."

"Not me, Your Excellency," said Father Baker quickly, "but Our Lady of Victory. She is the one who saw to the financing and the building, and all congratulations should go to her."

Bishop Turner knew of Father Baker's "holy city of charity" at Lackawanna, N. Y., on the outskirts of Buffalo, and he had long since ceased to be amazed at what Father Baker could accomplish with the aid of Our Lady of Victory. But this was Father Baker's crowning achievement — this marvelous church dedicated to Our Lady of Victory, completed in this year of 1926, and entirely free of debt so that it could be consecrated.

3

Father Baker's gentle voice brought him out of his musing. "Would the 25th of May be satisfactory, Bishop?"

"Oh. Oh, yes," said Bishop Turner. "Of course." And he jotted a note on his calendar for that day.

Father Baker and the charitable institutions at Lackawanna were almost synonymous in the minds of the public; yet they had existed for many years before he came there in 1876. Except for one short interval, Father Baker was at the institutions for more than sixty years — more than the lifetime of many persons. And under his wise and careful administration, Our Lady of Victory Homes had grown to national and international fame.

There were but three small buildings when Father Baker first came to Lackawanna, then known as Limestone Hill: St. Patrick's Church where the new Our Lady of Victory Basilica now stands, St. Joseph's Orphan Asylum on the opposite side of the street, and St. John's Protectory alongside the church.

But this year of 1926 had seen an amazing growth. Next to St. Joseph's Orphan Asylum stood the infant home, established to care for unwed mothers and their children.

Next to the infant home stood the shed protecting Father Baker's gas well — a "miracle," as many claimed, because he had persisted in drilling it against the advice of many experts, and had struck gas when all others had given up hope.

On the same side of the street stands Our Lady of Victory General Hospital, which serves a large part of the surrounding area with excellent medical care and still carries on Father Baker's tradition of helping the needy.

Almost directly across the street stands St. John's Protectory, to which Father Baker added so much as to make it almost an entirely new building, with its many training programs and activities for boys.

Many a priest would justly feel a sense of satisfaction at having accomplished a portion of what Father Baker had

4

done. Yet, far from feeling satisfied, he had embarked on his most ambitious project of all — the Our Lady of Victory Church, which he intended as a beautiful crown for his beloved patron. It is, indeed, a magnificent crowning achievement, but perhaps even more pleasing to Our Lady of Victory and to her divine Son was Father Baker's work for souls, the boys who came under his care, the unwed mothers he aided, the babies he gave to loving homes or brought to manhood in his homes of charity, the sick and afflicted he cared for in his hospital.

The life that was responsible for these wondrous works of charity started in the 1840's in the then small city of Buffalo. Father Baker, unfortunately, seems to have been unusually reticent about his family life, his early childhood, even about his experiences as a young man and as a young priest.

One such incident concerns his service as a Union soldier during the Civil War. The only evidence or even hint of such service was a casual remark which someone interpreted as meaning that Father Baker had been a drummer boy during that struggle between the North and the South. It was much more than that. He was a member of the New York State militia, served with the Army of the North near Gettysburg during that climactic battle, and later helped put down the bloody draft riots in New York City. Apparently, never a word of this was told by Father Baker, even to his surviving close relatives. The true record was established only by digging through military documents, consulting the National Archives in Washington, etc.

One might outline several reasons for this seeming reluctance to talk about himself. Father Baker was not a close-mouthed clam. He was friendly, approachable, and charming, even to those who met him but once. One priest in the Buffalo diocese relates that, shortly before he was born, his parents had a casual contact with Father Baker. They had no particular problem. They had not come with a difficulty to be solved, as so many did. But Father Baker's personality made such an impact that when their son was born, he was given the first name of Nelson. There is a mystery as to how Father Baker was given the first name of Nelson. There is none as to why so many men in the Buffalo area bear it today. Their parents had some contact with the famed Father Nelson H. Baker of Lackawanna, and named their sons after him.

Father Baker talked to individuals, to small groups, to large gatherings, and talked exceedingly well. Again, however, he did not talk about himself, nor indulge in personal reminiscences. He talked about what we could call his work, but what he called Our Lady of Victory's work. Unceasingly, in and out of season, he did the work to which he felt he was called by our Lord, through His Mother, Our Lady of Victory, and everything else faded into obscurity.

He maintained close relationships with his mother and father during their lifetimes, and with his brothers and their children. While he would at times reminisce with his brothers about their childhood pranks and activities, he seemed never to have done this with others, nor written about it in any of his publications.

Even the date of his birth is not completely certain. The year has been given as 1841, 1842, and even 1850. It seems very likely that Father Baker did not consider birthdays very important — his birthdays, that is. Brother Stanislaus, one of his zealous helpers with the boys and the first editor of The Victorian, recalls that when Father Baker was ninety years old, one of the many societies helping him gave a party. They presented him with many gifts, one a little tree with a number of bills in various denominations fastened to it. Father Baker looked at the tree, with all the money represented on it, and said, "All that on account of being ninety years old? If I knew there was so much money to it, I would have had that birthday long ago!"

The records of the Buffalo chancery office show his birth

6

date as February 16, 1842. This is substantiated by the records of New York State. The Office of the Adjutant General in Albany shows Nelson Baker's age as 21 when he enlisted in the New York State Volunteer Militia on June 19, 1863, for service during the Civil War.

The use of 1841 as the year of his birth probably stems from the fact that when he was baptized in St. Patrick's Church, Buffalo, on November 29, 1851, his age was recorded as ten. However, if he were born on February 16, 1842, he would have lacked two and a half months of being ten years old.

Nelson's mother was Irish Catholic. She was born on March 17, 1817; died on September 30, 1885; and lies buried beside her famous son in Holy Cross Cemetery. She had a tremendous influence on Nelson, one that lasted throughout his entire life. Although Father Baker was extremely reticent about his family, he did make one reference during a sermon on St. Patrick's day: "I thank God for having raised me to the dignity of the Catholic priesthood through the influence of an Irish Catholic mother."

Nelson was the second son of Lewis and Caroline Donnellan Baker. His older brother, Lewis P., had been born in 1839 — and one naturally wonders, since Mrs. Baker was born on St. Patrick's day, whether her first child bore the middle name of that favorite Irish saint. There were four children in the Baker family, all boys: Lewis P.; Nelson; Andrew, who was born in 1845; and Ransom, in 1846.

The father, Lewis Baker, first appears in the Buffalo city directory in 1842, with his occupation shown as a mariner. His home was listed as at Oak and South Huron, which in later years was more specifically shown as 150 Oak Street. That is probably where Nelson was born.

At that time, Buffalo had been a city for less than ten years. In 1842 its population was probably a little more than 20,000, a busy, bustling big city for the times. The opening of the Erie Canal in 1825 had given the Great Lakes area a shipping outlet by water to the East and to the Atlantic Ocean. The canal had brought many people into the Buffalo area, first to dig it, and then to handle the increased industry that resulted from its completion. There were many European immigrants during that period, particularly from Germany. Possibly Nelson Baker's father was one of these. This seems substantiated by the fact that Nelson spoke German fluently.

By 1858 at least, and perhaps earlier, Lewis Baker had become a businessman on his own account. He opened a grocery and general store on Batavia Street in Buffalo, which is now Broadway, between Hickory and Walnut Streets. The family lived behind the store. In the rooms above the store, the local Republican organization had its offices, with a flag prominently so designating. Down the street was the Democratic headquarters. They too had a proud banner flying.

One summer there was considerable political activity, with men gathering at both headquarters, so much so that it attracted the attention of Nelson and his younger brother, Ransom. Nelson's active mind hatched a scheme, which he confided under deep secrecy to his younger brother.

That night was dark, with the moon half hidden by the clouds. Every now and then, the moon's light broke through, and lit up the plank road that was the pride of Batavia Street.

Most everyone had long since gone to sleep — everyone, that is, except the two small boys, who had pulled trousers over their nightshirts and were now cautiously inching their way along the wall of Baker's General Store.

Just as they reached the corner, the smaller boy grabbed the older by the arm. "Nelson!" he whispered.

"Shhh!" said Nelson.

"Nelson! What if Pa catches us?"

"You keep making noise, Ransom, and he sure will catch us." Nelson paused a minute. "I guess he'd just about skin us alive if he caught us. So we'd better not let him. Now be quiet, Ransom."

The two boys tiptoed over to the flagpole which stood in

8

front of the Baker store. Nelson quickly untied the rope and lowered the Republican flag. Folding it, he tucked it under his arm and led the way to the Democratic flagpole. There he handed the Republican flag to Ransom, took down the Democratic one — and soon the double switch of flags was accomplished. Then quietly, softly, the two boys made their way to the back door of the store, to the family's living quarters, to slip back into their room and into bed.

Just before they reached the door, Nelson held up a warning hand and said, "Listen, Ransom. If Pa or Ma wake up and ask what we're doing, say we want a drink of water. Then take a drink of water — so you won't be lying." But the two boys made their way safely to their bed and soon were sleeping soundly, the sleep of the innocent and the just.

After breakfast the next morning, Ransom wanted to go out in front of the store "to see what was happening." But Nelson held him back, saying, "We don't usually go out front to play till we get our chores done — somebody might notice that. Let's do everything just as usual." And so they did, for Nelson was the leader in activities of the Baker children, especially where Ransom was concerned.

So they busied themselves about the back of the store, bringing in wood for their mother and doing their other chores. Then, suddenly, an uproar of shouts and the scuffling of feet was heard out on the street. The two boys raced for the front of the store. Lewis Baker, their father, was out in front too, a white apron tied around his waist.

"What happened, Pa?" asked Nelson, as he and Ransom joined him.

"Someone changed the Republican and Democratic banners."

Three or four men were shoving and scuffling around the base of the Republican flagpole. Then two of the men squared off with their fists, and Ransom yelled, "Fight! Fight!" as he danced nearer.

"None of that!" cried Mr. Baker sternly as he marched

9

over to the flagpole and separated the men. "Do you want the constable down here, and the two of you hauled off to jail for a few days?"

"Those blasted Democrats put their flag on our flagpole!"

"Those blasted Republicans put their flag on our flagpole!"

"Now, now, none of that," said Mr. Baker. "Some practical joker is probably having the time of his life, watching you men act like boys. Take the flags down, exchange them — and hope the editor of the paper doesn't find out about it, or you'll be the laughingstock of Buffalo."

Lewis Baker let his eyes rove over the crowd and then reflectively settle on Nelson and Ransom as he thoughtfully stroked his chin. Nelson pretended not to see the question in his father's eyes. Aside to Ransom he said, "Race you to the bell tower!" And they ran down the street toward the water front, where the bell was hung to call the men to fires.

CHAPTER II

NOT too much is known about the religious life of Nelson Baker as a boy and a young man, though there has been much conjecture. The records of St. Patrick's Church of Buffalo show that he was baptized by the Rev. Joseph Lennon on November 29, 1851, with Father Lennon and Ann Brooks as sponsors.

It is not definitely known whether Nelson's brothers were baptized as Catholics. However, there is some indirect evidence that they may have been. Shortly before the oldest brother, Lewis P., died in 1922, Monsignor Baker tried to hear his confession and to anoint him. Naturally he would not have done this if his brother had not been baptized a Catholic. Monsignor Henry B. Shaw, who is now the pastor of Holy Family Church in Buffalo, and was then an assistant to Monsignor Baker at Lackawanna, recalls the incident.

"We were coming home from the chancery office one day, and we stopped at the house where Father Baker's brother lived. Father Baker said that he was going to try to hear his brother's confession and anoint him, and he went into the house. Of course I waited in the car outside.

"Father Baker soon came out, very agitated, and said, 'I wasn't able to do anything. I put on my stole and went in, and told my brother that it would be nice if he would go to confession and I would anoint him. At that particular moment my brother's wife came in and said, "Nelson Baker,

11

what are you trying to do? You can't give any blessing to him." So I took off my stole and went out.' "

Monsignor Shaw recalls that Father Baker was very much agitated to think of it. He said, "It was too bad that I put on my stole. That way they saw what I was doing."

Another brother, the youngest, Ransom, died in 1930. Monsignor Baker celebrated a Solemn Requiem Mass for the repose of his soul in Our Lady of Victory Basilica at Lackawanna, though the body was interred in Forest Lawn, which is not a Catholic cemetery.

The third brother, Andrew M., died suddenly in Long Beach, California, in 1933. He was unmarried and was found dead in his hotel room, having apparently died while preparing for bed.

All the Bakers had long lives. Monsignor Baker himself was 94 when he died on July 29, 1936. Andrew was 88, Ransom 84, and Lewis 83 at the time of their deaths.

There are many stories about Nelson Baker's early religious life. Some say that he would go with his mother to the six o'clock Mass on Sundays, and then the father would make the children go to a Protestant Sunday school and to Protestant church services later in the day. Others say that Mr. Baker did not much care which church the children attended, so long as they went to church. It was evident, however, that Nelson preferred to go to the Catholic church, and presumably he made his First Communion and was confirmed.

Generally, his life was quiet and peaceful. He was not very tall and always slight of figure. Yet he had a lively interest in baseball and the other sports he was able to play, and had a good voice for singing and some skill with musical instruments. He went to Public School No. 12, and then to Old Central High in Buffalo. He was graduated at 17 and went to work for his father in the store, the same as his older brother Lewis a few years earlier. Nelson had a quick mind and was good with figures, and his family felt he would do quite well in the business world. He saved his money, perhaps was even thinking of going into business for himself, when the Civil War broke out.

The people of Buffalo for some time had been helping Negro slaves escape from the Southern states into Canada. Buffalo was one of the foremost terminal stations on the "underground railroad," which helped the slaves make their way north. In June of 1863, General Robert E. Lee and his army swept into southern Pennsylvania. Rumors spread throughout Buffalo that the rebel troops were headed that way, and New York State called for 20,000 new militia.

Recruiting tents had been put up in front of churches, by the post office, and in other prominent spots around the city. And soon Nelson H. Baker was signing his name to enlistment papers. He had joined Company A of the 74th New York State Regiment of Militia as a private. That very night of June 18, 1863, he went into service.

The next morning Nelson Baker lined up with the rest of his comrades in arms, still dressed in his civilian clothes, for there were not enough uniforms to go around.

The whole Baker family had come down to see him off, for the militia was leaving immediately by train for Harrisburg. The government was still worried that General Lee would break through the Northern lines and come surging into New York State. Nelson could see his mother, worried, but trying not to show it; his father, proud, and trying not to show that either; and his brothers, dancing with excitement as he marched along to the railroad station. He gave them a last wave of good-by and boarded the coaches for the thirty-hour dusty ride to Harrisburg.

On arrival, the men immediately marched to Camp Curtin, about two miles away. Nelson could see that the shutters had been taken down from the store windows and that merchants were open for business, and he assumed that the immediate danger was gone. Later he managed to talk to one of the Pennsylvania soldiers, and learned that the Southern forces had retreated from the area and gone to Williamsport.

13

Quickly the men received their uniforms, their rifles, and then moved to Mount Union, Pennsylvania, where Company A was put on picket duty.

The lieutenant in charge of Company A called for volunteers for the first night's duty, and Nelson Baker stepped forward among the first. The officer told the men the importance of their guard duty, that near the camp the Pennsylvania Railroad crossed the Juanita River over a $1,000,000 bridge, and that the aqueduct of the Pennsylvania Canal also crossed the river there.

"If the enemy could destroy these, he could cut off all communication between Pittsburgh and Harrisburg," he emphasized. "We must use the utmost vigilance."

The first night was quiet, as Nelson watched carefully to see that no enemy soldiers came through their lines. The second night had its excitement, however.

There was a bright moon that flooded the clearings in the woods, but it was dark — and looked dangerous — under the trees throughout Nelson's patrol area. He had been on duty for some time when he heard someone shoving his way through the underbrush.

The noise moved nearer, became even louder. Nelson was suspicious. This might be a trap to get him out into the open. Cautiously he moved in the direction of the noise. Then, as he pushed into a clearing, he saw a Southern soldier stumbling along, holding his left shoulder. Nelson looked around to see if the man was alone, but he could see no one else. Stepping behind a large tree to protect himself in case there were others, he called, "Halt! Halt — or I'll fire!"

The man abruptly stopped. "Don't shoot!"

"Who are you?" Nelson Baker asked.

"From General Imboden's cavalry. I'm wounded, my horse was shot, and I got separated from our army."

"Are you alone?"

"Yes. Help me, please . . ." and then the Southerner slumped to the ground.

14

Cautiously Nelson went forward and saw that the man seemed to have fainted from loss of blood. Stopping the flow, he revived the man and brought him to other members of the company, who took him into camp.

There were other stragglers from the Southern army who wandered into the picket lines and were captured, but generally the guard duty was quiet. On the night of July 2, however, the regiment commander sent Company A and Company D on a forced march to the Mill Creek railroad bridge. General Imboden reportedly had 500 cavalrymen ready to attack it, and the Union soldiers were rushed there to defend the bridge.

When the soldiers arrived at the mountain passes, Nelson Baker quickly saw how easily the Confederate soldiers could be stopped. The road was a narrow one, with barely room for four men to ride abreast. Scouts had been sent to enlist the aid of farmers, who met the soldiers at the pass.

After the Union soldiers marched into the pass, the farmers cut down trees to block the road at that end, so the Confederate cavalrymen could not escape from the trap planned for them.

Then Nelson Baker and some other soldiers were sent with more farmers to the end of the pass where the Imboden cavalry would enter the guarded area. The farmers cut some trees nearly through, so that a few sharp blows would send them toppling into the road, trapping the Confederates in a box, with the Union soldiers right alongside.

Nelson Baker climbed a tree and watched Bear Valley for signs of action. About 2 a.m., he began to notice movement of horses, and so reported to his officers on the ground. Nelson saw the cavalrymen come to a stop, the horses milling around in a clearing for a few minutes as a group of officers talked to some men on foot. Then an officer at the head of the troops waved his sword, glittering in the moonlight, turned his horse around, and headed in the opposite direction.

After he reported this to the lieutenant in charge of Com-

15

pany A, Nelson asked a farmer if there were another pass nearby. "Would they try that, do you think?" he asked.

"Likely not," said the farmer. "They've got friends around here too, just as the Union has. Probably someone told them you was waitin' for 'em. They knew they wouldn't have a chance in these narrow roads through the pass."

The Union soldiers waited under the trees until daybreak, and then began the march back to camp. On the Fourth of July, 1863, they were officially sworn into the service of the United States. Nelson Baker felt he couldn't have been prouder, as he stood, ramrod erect, with head uncovered and hand upraised, in front of the colonel's tent.

The rest of the day was spent in ease and quiet. In the evening, the men sat around, talking of Buffalo and singing old songs together. They had named their streets after those in Buffalo, and Nelson's tent was on Batavia. He borrowed a guitar from a neighboring tent, and his fine tenor voice led the others in singing the familiar old songs.

The next day another "hurry-up" marching order was received. The Confederates were retreating after the disastrous battle at Gettysburg, and the 74th Regiment was sent to Maryland. The forced march was a brutal one. The roads were in dreadful condition from heavy rains, and the men had to jump from stone to stone to avoid the knee-deep mud. Nelson looked frail and small, but he was wiry and in good physical condition. He crawled along the tops of fences to cross some of the flooded spots on the road, and managed to make the trip without much difficulty. Some of the others, however, trying to follow him, slipped off and plopped into the mud and water, to the amusement of their fellow soldiers.

Finally, on July 9, the 74th Regiment arrived within two miles of Clear Spring, Maryland, and camped for the night. The next morning scouts brought back word that Union cavalrymen were having a skirmish with the Southern soldiers.

The officers snapped their orders — "Advance — double quick!" — and Nelson rushed forward with the others, his

16

Springfield ready for fast use if necessary. However, when the Southern soldiers saw the larger Union force approaching, they decided to retreat and left the field to the 74th Regiment.

They camped near a mountain called "Fairview." As they began to set up the tents, the lieutenant called Nelson and a few other soldiers aside. "Our scouts report that General Lee's army is nearby, and is crossing the Potomac River just a few miles away. I want you to go to the top of the mountain and try to see just where the Southern troops are, and how many. I don't suppose I need tell you to be careful."

Nelson led the men up the side of the mountain, carefully watching for any Southern scouts. They found none; and when they reached the top, they found out why. The Confederates were too busy ferrying their troops across the river below. Nelson shinnied up a tree and carefully studied the movement of the troops.

"How many do you think there are?" one of the soldiers asked.

"Ten thousand anyway — about two and a half miles from here. It looks like General Imboden's cavalry. He's got cavalry, infantry, and artillery. He could wipe us out without much trouble if he came after us. They've got many more men than we do." And so he reported to the lieutenant when they returned to camp.

"How about General Lee's army?" the lieutenant asked.

"They're crossing the Potomac in boats, and farther down, in what looks like a shallow part, they are building pontoon bridges."

"Pontoon bridges? Where did they get the material for that?"

"Looks as though they're using pieces of houses and old canal boats — anything that'll float."

Quickly, the colonel commanding the 74th Regiment sent out four companies to guard against a surprise attack, and warned the soldiers to use the greatest vigilance.

The Union soldiers were on a constant alert until their relief arrived during the night of July 11 and the morning of July 12. This was General Kelley's division, and he immediately posted a battery of artillery on the mountain and began shelling Imboden's army.

Later in the day, General Kelley inspected the 74th Regiment and complimented the men on their fine appearance. "You could not have done your work better," he told them. The general rode away, but suddenly turned and came back to face Colonel Fox, commanding the 74th. "Colonel Fox," he said, "you and your regiment are a brave lot of men — or else a damned lot of fools who do not know the danger they were in."

CHAPTER III

THE 74th Regiment had been relieved. Its term of enlistment was only for thirty days and that time was nearly up. It looked as though the militia would soon be going home to Buffalo, since the emergency that brought them into service seemed over.

However, a new emergency arose. On Monday, July 13, the draft of men for the army had become effective. In New York City, the general feeling at first had been favorable toward the draft, but it soon changed. Riotous protest demonstrations started at ten Monday morning and raged until late at night, with assaults, murders, and buildings set on fire. At first only a few rowdies were involved; then others joined until the city and state authorities were almost completely helpless.

The mobs had turned particularly against the Negroes in the city, and were merciless in their attacks against them. Sometimes this was because of the color of their skin; but more often it was because the Negroes were working on the docks and in the factories, and some of the men in the mobs felt the Negroes were taking their jobs. The city was terrorized as the mobs ran wild, killing those they found on the streets, breaking into houses, destroying furniture, and burning buildings.

Again the 74th Regiment received rush orders, to report to New York City "with all possible dispatch." Again the men made a forced march, this time to Harrisburg, keeping

19

continuously on the road until they arrived at the railroad station. Their only rest was taken in snatches of a few hours, sleeping on muddy sidewalks in small towns or along the road.

The military train pushed through Pennsylvania and into New Jersey. At one of the towns, Nelson Baker slipped out to pick up a newspaper, and showed his fellow soldiers the headlines: EVENING MOB ARMED WITH RIFLES — MORE NEGROES HUNG. Nelson pointed to the headlines. "No wonder they've called for the national guard. This is just like war — but worse."

"That's why we're here, boys," said one of the officers who was going down the aisle. "What the Union is fighting for could easily be lost if this rioting continues."

When the 74th Regiment's train pulled into Jersey City, the town was quiet. The men quickly lined up to march to the ferry, which would bring them over the Hudson River to New York City. Nelson sought out one of the ferry workers. "How are things in New York City now?" he asked.

The man shrugged his shoulders, as he continued coiling the heavy rope. "Getting better, I think. The 7th went over last night, and so did the 65th, with a battery of guns. And I'll bet it gets better fast when all you fellows are over there. Them hoodlums don't want to face soldiers with guns."

When the ferry docked in New York, the officers formed the 74th Regiment into line. A crowd of rough-looking men had gathered at the dock, and Nelson could hear the muttered threats and curses as they watched the soldiers get into formation. Then came the sharp order, "Fix bayonets!" Swiftly, smoothly, the bright steel was fastened to the end of the long rifles, and some of the hoodlums nearby stepped back as they realized that the soldiers meant business. There were smiles, too, on the faces of others who welcomed the soldiers' arrival.

As the 74th Regiment marched down the center of the cobblestoned street, Nelson could see ahead, and on both sides, the broken windows, the doors battered in, furniture

20

thrown into the street and broken, even the smoldering embers of houses set afire during the night and not yet burned out. The soldiers were marched through some of the waterfront areas, as a clear warning to the rioting mobs that their rule of New York City had ended.

As they went down one street, the soldiers heard shouts and a few scattered shots around the next corner. "On the double!" shouted the officers, and the men of the 74th ran forward. Turning the corner, they saw a half-dozen Union soldiers and officers attacked by a mob armed with pistols and clubs. "Charge!" shouted Company A's lieutenant, and the men moved up, bayonets leveled. The mob stood for a moment, bewildered at the sudden change in the situation, and then broke and ran for their lives. One of the rescued officers said, "Thank God you came along. We were out surveying the situation, and all of a sudden they jumped us."

Company A stayed in New York City for about two days, but the back of the rioting had been broken. There was still some disturbance in the outlying areas, and Companies A and B were sent up the Hudson River as far as Sing Sing, where they stopped several riots before they had gone too far.

Finally, on July 21, 1863, the 74th Regiment left New York City for Buffalo, where they received a magnificent reception. There was a grand reunion in the Lewis Baker home, and Nelson had to tell all about his adventures to his proud mother and father and to his envious brothers.

One night, Joseph Meyer, a friend of Nelson's for some time, came to see him.

"Nelson," he said, "have you ever thought of going into business for yourself?"

Nelson Baker laughed, and he had a jolly laugh. "Oh, sure, lots of times."

"I'm not joking," said Joe Meyer. "I'm serious about this."

"Oh, I've thought about it," Nelson told him, "but I just don't know what I want to do."

"Now is the time," said Joe Meyer. "Buffalo is growing, and it's going to grow more. It will be a great metropolis some day. We've got a chance to get started in business and grow with the city."

Nelson looked at his friend sharply, then smiled and asked, "What do you mean — we?"

"We, you and I. Let's go into business together," said Meyer earnestly. "You've got a good business head, I know. And I think I have."

Nelson Baker turned the suggestion over in his mind a bit, while Meyer nervously waited, for he very much wanted his friend as a partner. "What business?" asked Nelson finally.

"That's more like it!" said Meyer with a smile. "The flour and feed business. There's a store over on Washington Street that's empty, and it'd be a good location."

Nelson held up his hands quickly. "Wait! Don't rush me, Joe. I'm not sure that this is what I want to do."

Joe Meyer got up and began pacing the floor in exasperation. Then he turned to Nelson. "Well, what do you want to do? Go on clerking in your father's store all of your life?"

"Don't get hot under the collar, Joe. You know better than that. I'm just not sure what I want to do with my life. I know I want to help the poor in some way."

"Well, aren't you doing that now? You're working regularly in the St. Vincent de Paul Society. Isn't that helping the poor?"

"Sure it is — but I don't know if it's enough." With a burst of confidence, Nelson Baker added, "I guess I'm trying to find out what God wants me to do with my life. Sometimes I think I'd like to be a priest. But then I know I haven't had the right schooling for it. My mother would like that, but I don't think my father would."

"But what do you want to do?"

Nelson Baker pulled on his nose as he thought about the matter. "As I said, I want to help people — but how to do it is the problem."

22

"If we prosper in business, as we should," Joe Meyer said, "you could help poor people much more than if you continue working in your father's store."

Nelson Baker laughed. "You always get back to that, don't you, Joe? Perhaps you're right." He stuck out his hand. "Partners it is, Joe — unless I find that God has other plans for me."

Joe Meyer shook Nelson Baker's hand happily, for he felt sure the two of them would be successful, and they were. Both were hard working, both good businessmen, and the partnership prospered during the coming years.

One day Nelson Baker was returning from a buying trip out in the country along the lake shore, when he came upon two boys carrying a heavy bag. He stopped his horse and wagon and called out, "Hop in, boys — there's plenty of room here."

The heavy bag was put into the wagon, and the boys climbed up onto the seat alongside the young businessman.

"How far are you going?" he asked.

"To Limestone Hill," the older boy answered.

"Do you live there?" Nelson asked.

"Now we do," the younger said. "We're brothers. We live at St. Joseph's Boys' Home."

"Oh, you do," said Nelson. "I know your Father Hines."

"Do you?" they said with a smile. "He let us go out for a hike 'cause it's my birthday," said the younger one, "and a farmer gave us a big bag of corn to bring back."

"What'll you do with the corn?" Nelson Baker asked.

"Oh, we can always use it," the older boy replied. "We need lots of food at St. Joseph's."

"Do you have enough?" Nelson Baker asked.

"Oh, sure," said the younger one. "We always get enough. Sometimes Father Hines isn't very hungry, or the Sisters, and then we get theirs too."

Nelson Baker was quietly thinking as they approached the

orphanage building at Limestone Hill, with the small church on the opposite corner. A bakery and grocery store were nearby, and he stopped his wagon there. He realized that the priest and Sisters of St. Joseph at the orphanage would sometimes go hungry — just so the boys would not.

"Wait a minute, boys," he said, "and I'll take you over to St. Joseph's. I want to see Father Hines, too."

He came out with a box and gave it to the younger boy. "This is a birthday cake for you, just to celebrate with." A clerk from the store came out with a bigger box and put it in the wagon, and then Nelson drove over to St. Joseph's.

As the boys went running into the orphan home, Father Hines came out. "Nelson Baker! It's nice to see you again."

"I picked up two of your boys, out for a hike, and I thought I'd drop in for a minute. Can you use some extra supplies I happen to have along?"

Father Hines gave Mr. Baker a quick look and then said slowly, "You know, Nelson, we can always use supplies. But you've got your own responsibilities, and you do so much for us already."

"God has given us some success in our work, and we're just paying back a little."

"We're always grateful to you for your help, and I'm sure our Lady is, for these are her children too. But come — see this new addition we're putting onto St. John's Protectory across the street."

"Where are you going to get all the boys to fill it?"

Father Hines smiled sadly. "I'm not worried about getting the boys, Nelson, and you know why. There are too many homeless Catholic boys with no proper place to go. But look, here is something new since the last time you were out. We're making our own bricks, the boys and I, with the help of some brickmakers we've hired, and we're doing some of the building ourselves."

"Father Hines, I'm amazed at how much you're able to do here — and with so little."

24

"It serves a double purpose, as you know," said Father Hines. "The boys learn a trade, which they will need when they go out on their own, and we get the bricks which we need for our building."

Nelson Baker looked at the big St. John's Protectory building, with the addition going up alongside. "Father," he said, "I know this is none of my business, but I hate to see those windows barred like that. You'd think this was a prison!"

Father Hines smiled and was not offended. "We've talked about this before, Nelson, and I know how you feel. But there are boys sent here by the courts because they've been in trouble. Some of them are bad boys —"

"There are no bad boys. There are neglected boys, mistreated boys, boys in trouble — but they aren't bad."

"I know you feel that way, Nelson. I don't quite agree with you, but that is the way institutions like this are built. Besides, the townspeople would scream if I took off those bars. They'd be afraid that the boys would ransack the town."

"They don't know any better, Father," Nelson Baker said thoughtfully, "but you do. And how are the boys going to have any faith in themselves — if no one else does? Especially if you don't?"

"I do have faith in them, Nelson, and I agree with you, but there's nothing I can do about it. But, say, I was down at the Jesuit rectory the other day, and Father Durthaller tells me you're studying Latin and other subjects in the evening. That's interesting. Any particular reason?" Father Hines's tone was casual, too casual, and Nelson had to laugh.

"Mind reading, Father?"

"Hoping instead, I think."

"I've thought for a long time I'd like to be a priest, and Father Durthaller assigned a young Jesuit to give me some time. So I've been studying to see if I could take it."

"And?"

"My mind is getting closer to a decision — but I still don't really know."

Father Hines studied this alert young businessman who had already made his mark in Buffalo, whose partnership was a very successful one, and whose charity to the poor and helpless was — in spite of his efforts — well known to many people.

"There's one sure way to find if you have a vocation, Nelson, if you really want to know."

"What is that?"

"If you apply to the Bishop and are accepted as a candidate. Have you talked to Bishop Ryan at all?"

"Oh, no. I've met the Bishop, of course — but I've never talked to him about it."

"Why don't you? I'd be glad to give you a note to him, and I can recommend you highly."

When Nelson Baker left Limestone Hill for the drive back to Buffalo, his head was so filled with thoughts of the possibility of becoming a priest that he stopped at the Bishop's residence on the way.

Bishop Ryan was most gracious as Nelson explained his hopes and his dreams. "Of course we'd be delighted to have you as a student for the priesthood," the Bishop said. "Many people have told me of your charity, of your desire to help the Church. However, I feel I must point out that the road is not easy. This will mean going back to school — after you have been a successful businessman. That's not easy, and you may have times of discouragement and despair. On the other hand, I am sure that our Lady and our Lord will help you over the rough spots; and, if you persevere, you will do great good for your fellow men."

"I know," said Nelson soberly. "I've been trying to decide what to do with my life. And I do want to help people in some way, if I can."

"Our seminary is Our Lady of the Angels, at Suspension Bridge, near the Falls. You could take your college courses there, and go right on. But I would want you to understand the hard work that is involved, especially since you've been away from school for a number of years. It may be difficult for a man of your age and experience to go to school with younger men."

Nelson Baker smiled. "Perhaps it will be an aid to my humility, Bishop Ryan."

The Bishop was pleased. "You have the right spirit, Mr. Baker. There is a tremendous need for priests in the Buffalo diocese. A man of your background could do really great work for God and for His Church. Believe me, if you decide to make application for the seminary, I shall do everything I can to help you, and I shall pray to God and His Blessed Mother that you may persevere."

CHAPTER IV

NELSON pondered the idea for a time, and then one morning in 1868 he broke the news to Joe Meyer. It hit his partner like a bombshell. He had completely forgotten their earlier talks, and when Nelson said, "Joe, I'm going to study for the priesthood," all Joe Meyer could say was, "You don't mean it!"

"Oh, yes, I do mean it."

"But you're too old to study for the priesthood! You're twenty-six already. You'll have to study Latin and all those subjects! You've been away from books for a long, long time."

"I know all that, Joe. I know it won't be easy. But the Bishop is willing to let me do it, and so I want to do it. I just hope that I can stick it out."

Meyer's hopes raised a bit at this. "And if you don't?"

Nelson Baker smiled a little. He had no thought of not sticking it out, and he intended to do all he could to attain his goal, but there was also the possibility that he might not be suited for it. "If I don't, Joe, believe me, I'd still want to be partners with you. The Jesuits at St. Michael's are going to help me. I've been studying with them nights to see how it would work out."

For a year Nelson Baker continued the grind of a full business day and then an evening full of study. When the summer of 1869 came, he was ready for a change, away from the books of all kinds, business and otherwise.

He had not been well. In his few remaining papers we find a reference to a diet given him by a Dr. Loersch, in May that year, and less than a month later he left Buffalo by steamer on a trip down the Great Lakes.

Whatever the reason, certainly he used the quiet trip for meditation and for prayer, to determine whether he had — as he so devoutly hoped — a vocation to the priesthood.

Prayer seems to have dominated his trip. In Detroit, for instance, he received Communion at a 6:30 a.m. Mass, then went to a High Mass at 10:30 in the same church. In the afternoon he attended vespers at a French church, and also visited a Redemptorist church — "A very neat church, with a new schoolhouse, the largest I ever saw, 4 stories high."

When the lake boat stopped at Mackinac, Nelson Baker "found a little church. . . . Stayed around until bells tolled for Mass." In Milwaukee, too, and in Chicago, he found his way to the Catholic churches and prayed there that he might make the right decision.

On the way back to Buffalo, the vessel stopped at a small Canadian village to take on wood for the boilers. Immediately Nelson Baker, as he wrote in his diary, "went into the village, heard the bells ring for Mass, started for the direction of the bell and had the extreme pleasure of hearing Mass in their little church . . . also went to conf. there and staid there until about noon when we started."

When he returned to Buffalo, his mind was clear and his decision made.

First he told his mother, as soon as he had an opportunity to be alone with her. "I talked to the Bishop today, and he said yes."

Her eyes brightened, but she asked quietly, "Yes to what?"

Nelson watched her closely as he replied, "Yes to my studying for the priesthood for the Buffalo diocese."

Her eyes filled with tears as she put her arms around him. "I've prayed for this," she whispered. "I've prayed for years and years. I always hoped one of my boys would be a priest, but the last few years it seemed as though you were the only one who might receive the grace to do it."

Nelson put his hands on his mother's shoulders and said soberly, "Listen, Mother. This will be hard, and I might not be able to finish the courses and be ordained. It's been a long time since I went to school."

His mother smiled. "Nelson, you've never failed in anything you put your heart and soul into. And I know you won't now. God wants you, and our Blessed Mother wants you — and I know you'll do great work for them."

He got a different reaction when he talked to his father. "Nelson, you're a grown man now," he said. "If you want to do this, certainly I can't object. But you should consider the whole matter very carefully. You have an excellent business with Joe Meyer. You've been making good money. You've got money in the bank. You might better be thinking about getting married and setting up your own home."

Nelson listened quietly to his father's comments, and listened too as his brothers added their own remarks in much the same vein. "I can see how you feel," he said finally, "and for many people that would be the right thing. But it isn't what I want to do."

Lewis Baker shook his head sorrowfully. "You have to follow your own conscience in this, Nelson," he said. "I hope you're not making a mistake, and I trust you'll not be sorry for it."

Nelson smiled. "I don't think I'll be sorry for it — even if it turns out that I can't make the grade. This way I'll know for sure either that I should or should not. That's better than going through the rest of my life wondering."

The next morning, as he went, bright and early, to the store of Meyer and Baker, he thought about Joe's reaction and he knew how it would be. Early in the day he found an opportunity to sit down with his partner. "Joe, I've got something important to talk to you about."

Meyer looked up, surprised. "What's wrong, Nelson?"

30

"Nothing's wrong — in fact, everything is right. Remember that talk we had last year, when I started studying at St. Michael's with the Jesuits?"

"Oh, no! You're not going to be a priest!"

"I hope I am. I'm going to try hard, and I'm going to Our Lady of the Angels Seminary at Suspension Bridge in September."

"Oh, no!" Joe Meyer was the picture of despair as he held his head in his hands. "You can't do this to me, Nelson — break up the partnership! I can't possibly raise the money now to buy out your share —"

"Wait a minute," said Nelson. "Don't jump off the bridge, Joe."

"You're the one that's jumping. I'm the one that's going to sink."

"Listen to me. We don't have to break up the partnership. The firm can still be Meyer and Baker. I can get my brother Ransom to come here and take my place. I'll leave my money in the partnership. Then, if you and Ransom get along well, I can sell my share to him — and you'll have your partner and your business."

Meyer thought a few minutes and then said with a rueful smile, "I might have known you'd have it all figured out. Ransom would be good — though not as good as you, Nelson. Any chance of talking you out of it?"

Nelson Baker laughed. "Not a chance!"

Meyer nodded. "I know — or should have known. When are you going to leave?"

"I'm due there on September 2. I haven't talked to Ransom yet about this, because I wanted to know how you felt. But I'll do that tonight. I'm sure he'd welcome the chance to go into business with you."

"I'm still sorry, Nelson. We've got along wonderfully these five years. I'd rather have you as a partner than anyone I know."

"I'm sorry too, Joe. But this is something I have to do."

On September 2, 1869, Nelson entered the college department of Our Lady of the Angels Seminary at Suspension Bridge, which is now part of Niagara Falls. He fitted quickly into the life of the college, even though he was considerably older than most of the students. He noted in his college diary that he "got acquainted very easily with some of the boys."

His first few days were taken up with getting familiar with the college and into the school's routine. He wrote in his diary for September 3: "In morning arranged and selected our little beds, and decorated our little place with some holy pictures."

Later in the week, as more of the students arrived, he wrote: "Had a good game of football, and also of catching about an hour, and went in field with John and helped him dig potatoes for dinner." No lack of physical energy there, despite his slight frame.

This was not an easy thing that Nelson Baker had done, considering his age and the great change it was from his customary life. But he also experienced a certain mental turmoil because he knew that many of his friends thought he was being extremely foolish to attempt to attain the priesthood at that late age. This is shown by a brief notation in his diary for January 29, 1870, after he had been at Our Lady of the Angels but four months: "Father, I think, does not like to have me here, nor my partner nor brothers, but my mother and God and Mary do." It is amply evident, from his long life in the service of God, his devotion to Our Lady of Victory, and his love for his own mother, whose wishes Nelson Baker followed.

He was conscious, however, of the many problems he faced, and set down for himself rules for self-discipline. In his college diary, he made these notes just a few days after coming to Our Lady of the Angels:

Rules laid down by me, Nelson H. Baker, which I intend to keep and follow out to the letter, with the help of Thy divine grace, O my God, and the help of thy powerful assistance, O my Queen, this 16th day of September, 1869. I will firmly promise not to violate them. Amen.

1st. I will go to Holy Communion every Sunday morning at 6 o'clock Mass.

2nd. While in college I will never miss 8½ o'clock Mass.

3rd. I will always assist at vespers, Benediction, and all prayers.

He made determined efforts — and undoubtedly successful ones — to control his appetite. There is nothing to suggest that this may have been a problem for him. Quite likely Nelson Baker set down and followed these rules as a means of self-discipline, subjecting his body to his will, so that he might better subject himself to the will of God in future years. How successful he was we may judge by his success in the service of God and Our Lady of Victory — which was certainly spectacular. Later in 1869, Nelson Baker set down these rules for himself in his little college diary:

With Thy help, O God, and the help of Thy intercession, O Holy Mary my Queen, I hope to receive sufficient grace, to avoid *sin*, and this most detestable vice of *Gluttony*. Assist me to conform to these little rules, and not to be controlled by my wicked passions.

Breakfast.

Oatmeal and 2½ slices Graham bread or four oatmeal cakes. No drink.

Dinner.

Cracked wheat, 2½ slices Graham or 4 oatmeal cakes or little meat and potatoes & vegetables — or little soup & bread.

Supper.

2 pieces Graham and oatmeal or soak bread in tea and pour off tea & eat bread.

Apparently Nelson Baker felt he had a problem in disciplining himself, for again he set down rules for himself, this time on October 1, 1869, but only for a period of ten days. His diary records:

Rules. God help me. Pray.
I will eat no more Peaches.
 " "   " "   "   Pie.
 " "   " "   "   Custard.
 " "   " "   "   Bread pudding.
 " "   " "   "   "   "   sauce.
 " "   " "   "   Cakes.
 " "   " "   "   Tomatoes.
 " "   " "   "   Molasses.

His subjects in the college department were Latin, German, Algebra, Grammar, Catechism, History, and Declamation — and he did very well, notwithstanding his lack of previous training. In the first year of his schooling, he won first honors in German and Declamation, and "first *accesserunt*" in the other subjects. Accesserunt means, freely translated, that "they almost made it," or were runners-up to the top students.

CHAPTER V

OUR LADY OF THE ANGELS SEMINARY had begun its work on Nelson Baker, to fashion him for his divine vocation to the priesthood; and — perhaps naturally enough — Nelson Baker had already begun to make his contribution to his lifelong vocation of helping others.

He had been a student at the seminary for only a month when he was named to a student office. He noted in his diary that he was elected treasurer of "the Soc. of O. L. of Angels. We debate every week."

This was most likely the Literary Association, organized on October 6, 1869, with Nelson Baker as one of its charter members. The association had the object of instructing its members "in the correct management of like associations," and "also to furnish them with practical exercises in all the English branches." The college prospectus in later years noted that "strict attention is paid to elocution, debating, composition and declamation."

The fact that Nelson Baker was named an officer of the Literary Association in its first year of organization would seem to indicate that he had quite a hand in its formation, that his evident leadership and ability had been recognized by the younger men. Certainly he had quickly taken an active part in college life. As by dint of hard study he had gained an impressive standing scholastically, so by his graciousness and friendliness he did the same socially. Spiritually, he had progressed as well. Just four months after he entered the college, he formed the boys into an association for the Perpetual Adoration of the Most Blessed Sacrament. The diary of Our Lady of the Angels Seminary contains this notation under the date of January 6, 1870: "An association for the perpetual adoration of the Most Blessed Sacrament was organized — the members are college boys. Mr. Nelson Baker started and gave shape to this organization."

The association kept perpetual adoration by having two students remain in turn one quarter of an hour before the altar during the entire day. Nelson Baker had arranged this so that it did not interfere with studies or classes. During the adoration, the students were to pray for the conversion of sinners, especially those for whose salvation they might afterward be called to labor. In this, Nelson Baker was far ahead of his times. Nocturnal adoration was not then a widespread devotion in the United States.

Just a month later, in February, 1870, he was active in the formation of the high-sounding Philharmonic and Dramatic Association, being named its vice-president. The association's purpose was purely entertainment, and Nelson Baker was rated high among its talented members. Less than a month after its organization, the P.D.A. presented a program on Washington's birthday. As one looks over the program for the entertainment, he finds Nelson Baker singing a solo in the first part of the program, "Would I Were a Star." The second part included varieties on the theme of "Washington Crossing the Delaware" — and there too was N. H. Baker. Then came a medley on guitar, violin, and flute — together with Nelson H. Baker, who was quite proficient on the guitar.

The conclusion of the P.D.A. entertainment featured a "Laughable Farce," especially written for the occasion, entitled "Prince Arthur's Reception." Nelson Baker played a prominent part.

Within the month, the P.D.A. members trod the stage boards again, this time with a "serio-comic play, adapted

36

(they reported) from the original of Chow-chow, Tsi-Kiang, and presented now for the first time on any stage and entitled PHASES OF CITY LIFE." Again Nelson H. Baker was in the cast. The same group also formed the P.D.A. Glee Club, with Nelson H. Baker as the tenor and entertaining at many a student meeting.

Truly Nelson Baker was a versatile student. He stood high in his classes; he was a charter member of the Total Abstinence Society; he was one of the first prefects of the college sodality — and was also one of the rollicking black-faced comedians of the minstrel shows!

During 1871 the college Cecilian Association had given a "grand concert" for the students — elevating, no doubt, and musically quite successful, but hardly crowd-pleasing so far as the students were concerned. Then Nelson Baker was called upon to sing, which he did, with the then popular ballad of "I'm a Young Man From the Country." He was cheered lustily by the students who demanded an encore. He sang another lively tune — and this time the applause was even louder than before, with feet joining hands to the thundering demand for "another."

One of the students at the seminary wrote of the incident in his diary: "Suddenly Father Kavanagh, stung into action by the prolonged calls for Mr. Baker, started to his feet and exclaimed, 'That's insubordination,' or something to that effect. Scarcely were the words uttered ere Father Rice with indignation traced in every feature, turned toward the students and in tones not the most pleasant, said, 'We'll have none of this.'"

That ended Nelson Baker's encores, but it showed, dramatically and effectively, that he could please a crowd, and even stir it to action, with his pleasing songs.

The same college diary, which was written by the Rev. J. J. Mallen while he was at Our Lady of the Angels, described a speech that Nelson Baker gave on Washington's birthday in 1871:

"Mr. Baker selected for his discourse a dilation on the progress of our country since the days of Washington. He gave a lucid and precise history of the brilliant success which attended the country, the foundation of whose existence as a country had been so well laid by Washington.

"He showed how meagre were the resources of the infant republic during Washington's presidency and also the rapid increase under the prudent sway of still more prudent leaders. He wound up by expressing his desire and hope that this great republic which was now, in truth, the Rome of modern times, might not, like its ancient predecessor, fall, at length, on account of its own immense weight."

Father Mallen described Nelson Baker's address as a "masterly" production which conferred "great honor" on him.

Nelson was doing well in his studies. His diary notes in June, 1871: "Examination today. I spoke before Bishop Ryan and many other clergy — 'The Young Man of the Period,' rec'd 1st prize — declam. 1st."

That November, sitting in his little room, he wrote in his diary that he was "doing pretty well, better than some, thank God and Mary."

He was "doing pretty well" on the spiritual level; certainly he was not neglecting his duties in that regard. Those in the collegiate department were required to receive Communion "once every two weeks; and oftener if their directors deem proper. . . ." However, Nelson Baker was receiving our Lord in the Most Blessed Sacrament much more frequently than that — and this, of course, was long before the custom of daily Communion was encouraged for the layman. He wrote in his diary in 1871 that "I have the very great pleasure of going Saturday, Sunday and Wednesday — and our good Father Rice said I could go another day — I think I will go Thursday that I may obtain a greater love for our dear Lord in M. B. Sacrament."

He was to have great need for his growing spirituality, because that same year he received a heavy cross — a long siege of sickness that would have broken a less strong man, and perhaps even weakened the faith of many.

The illness that was almost to take Nelson Baker's life struck during November, 1871. He wrote about it very simply in his diary, probably because he was suffering so much that it was painful even to set down these simple details: "I was taken sick with erysipelas and had Doctors —— and —— but they did not help me, but rather injured me by bad treatment. Dr. Cronyn came down four times and helped me greatly."

Just how serious Nelson Baker's sickness was is shown by another letter, written by a classmate on December 20, 1871. It was written home by William F. Markoe, of White Bear Lake, Minnesota, during the time of this illness, and was later sent to *The Victorian*, Father Baker's magazine, and published in its issue of March, 1924. Mr. Markoe wrote:

"For several weeks we have had two boys at the point of death. One has been half devoured by erysipelas; but seems to be out of danger now. He is one of the two whom I mentioned in one of my first letters as being real saints, and he was looked upon as such by the whole house. . . .

"I had the pleasure of sitting up with him night before last, and I can assure you I heard a saint talk. You can hardly imagine what it is to hear him talk.

"He told me how intensely happy it made him feel to see the doctor shake his head dubiously, and to hear Father Rice say something about 'resignation'; and now that he is recovering, he speaks of being resigned to the will of God, and of being willing to live to please Him, as if it were as hard for him to live as it is for most men to die!

"He was despaired of and was anointed last Tuesday evening a week ago. The next morning there was a general Communion for him, and from that time he has been steadily improving."

There was no doubt about it. God had other plans for Nelson Baker. He was to have more than sixty years of active service for God and His Blessed Mother.

However, even though he was much better on that December 20, the end of his suffering was nowhere near. Nelson Baker was sick for several weeks at Our Lady of the Angels, critically sick. His closeness with his family — even though his father and brothers may not have approved of his "giving up" a career as a businessman — is shown by his diary notation that "Pa and Ma came down very often, and Ran and Andy and Lewis."

Then, when his condition continued critical, he was taken to the Sisters of Charity hospital in Buffalo. He very briefly summarized eleven weeks of pain and suffering by these few words in his diary: "When getting worse I was brought in a bed in the cars to Buffalo Hospital of S. of Char. Staid there eleven weeks, received some good care from Dr. Cronyn and the Sisters. Leg was opened eleven places — some lanced and some broken themselves. Paid Sisters one doll. pr. day — $68."

Nelson Baker received a full cup of intense suffering, for the treatment of erysipelas was excruciatingly painful — but he had offered it up to God; he desired only to do what God wanted him to do. He would have been happy to die, but God wanted him to live.

It was not until Easter of 1872 that he was able to walk, and then only on crutches. Nelson Baker struggled with these for five weeks; then he was graduated to two canes. Even by July he was not able to walk well with only one cane, but he wrote, "Thank God I am doing well." Even that October, he still felt the effects of his long illness. He was still using one cane, and was able to walk only a little without it.

But by then he had cause for jubilation. He had been accepted for the seminary; as he wrote in his diary in July: "Was told by Rev. Rice to get my cassock and be at the sem. the first Wed. in Sept. (Laus Deo)."

Because of his illness, he had been exempted from Scripture and Church History for the moment. He had, however, been studying hard, "4 or 5 hours a day," and felt that he was "doing pretty well — must study very hard."

Even though his body was weak, his determination was strong and his spirit willing. As he continued his studies in the seminary, he regained his strength — and with it, extended his activities. His organizational ability was often in evidence, as when he organized all the boys in an exhibition for St. Patrick's Day. He noted that "it took about 2 mos. to get it up, but it took first rate, though it nearly tired me out. I was some sick with a heavy cold on the 15th, was in bed most all day, but had to get up for the exhibition."

His spiritual growth, especially in humility, is shown by an incident during May, 1873. Two of the Vincentian Fathers who staffed Our Lady of the Angels Seminary were going to a general council, and Nelson Baker wrote in his diary, referring to one of them: "Fr. Lamey is to be the Prefect in his place. My self pride prompted to make me think that I would be acting officer, but it was a just humiliation for me to know that others had not as good an opinion of me, as I did myself. I thank God for this humiliation. I have prayed for this grace."

The following month he wrote: "Rev. P. V. K. is first Prefect but I do not like him so well as Fr. Landry, though he is a better disciplinarian. He is away a good deal and I must then control the boys — but I do not like to assume the authority, and I think they would learn to disrespect my authority in a very short time if he were away long. I thank God for destroying this *good opinion* of myself, thinking that I could manage them alone."

And he adds: "We have been examined. We all did well. I think I did remarkably well, better than expected. I studied hard for examinations . . . but I think Mr. Lopez was extra good to me."

In 1874, Nelson Baker read of a pilgrimage being organized from America to the famous shrines of Europe, the first of its kind. He had some money left from his business, and he wondered — would it be possible for him to go? For anyone who read the newspapers, it was not a good time to go to Europe. In Rome, Pope Pius IX had become the "prisoner of the Vatican" as the Italian soldiers had seized the property of the Holy See. The government was against the Catholic Church in France; and in Germany, Bismarck had thrown hundreds of priests into prison, and archbishops and bishops had also been arrested and put in jail. But Nelson Baker wasn't an ordinary person, so he went to the seminary rector.

"Father," he began, "have you read about the American pilgrimage to Europe?"

"Yes."

"Don't you think our seminary should be represented, that someone from here should go to Rome and pay our respects to the Holy Father?"

"That would be good," the rector agreed. "But the cost is $350 gold, and, Mr. Baker, I don't see how the seminary could spare the money."

"I realize that," Nelson said, "but I have some money left from my business. If it would be agreeable for me to go as the representative of the seminary, I would be happy to pay my own expenses."

The rector thought a moment or two, and then said, "The idea appeals to me, Mr. Baker, and if Bishop Ryan doesn't disapprove, I think it can be worked out. Suppose you take the cars into Buffalo and see the Bishop. I'll write him that you are coming and that we would have no objection."

The Bishop was most willing to have Mr. Baker go to Rome on the pilgrimage. "I know you will represent the seminary well," he told Nelson. "God go with you, and bring you safely home again."

The time seemed to fly by, and in May, 1874, Nelson left for New York City, to board the ship for Europe with the other pilgrims. He took with him a gift of $175 from the students and faculty of the seminary for the Holy Father, and a handsomely lettered scroll, also to be presented to the Pope.

CHAPTER VI

THE first American pilgrimage sailed from New York City on the French ship *Pereire*, which had just completed her one hundred and first crossing of the Atlantic. There were some fears among the fainthearted, for the French Transatlantic Line had just lost two of its steamers within a period of two weeks. But apparently the fainthearted had not signed for the pilgrimage, for one hundred and eight were on board, representing twenty-nine dioceses and vicariates apostolic of the relatively young Church in the United States.

New York City presented a different appearance to the 32-year-old seminarian than during the draft riots of 1863. Peace and quiet reigned, and the pilgrims were heartily welcomed by the Catholic societies of New York and New Jersey.

A special Mass for the pilgrims was celebrated on the morning of departure in St. Patrick's Cathedral in New York. A beautiful banner had been made for the journey, and Archbishop McCloskey formally blessed it.

Speaking to the pilgrims after he had celebrated Mass for them, Archbishop McCloskey praised their coming from all parts of the Union, "led by one common impulse, animated all by one common sentiment and thought and feeling, inspired all by one generous and noble and holy resolve, and that is to undertake what has never been undertaken before — a pilgrimage from these American shores of ours, a pilgrimage to Rome, a pilgrimage to the tombs of the Apostles, a pilgrimage to the feet of the Holy Father, to the shrine of the ever Blessed Mother Immaculate, made eminent the world over by the many blessings that have flowed from it, and to the shrine made glorious and consecrated by the graces that have been bestowed in such ample measure through the Sacred and Loving and Tender Heart of Jesus."

As he thrilled to the words of the Archbishop of New York, Nelson Baker thrilled even more to the prospects of the pilgrimage. Though he never told others of his reasons for making the pilgrimage, and indeed never told very many even that he was going, he undoubtedly had an additional motive of thanksgiving. He had been spared from a long and painful illness; and though he had bent his will to the will of God, he was grateful for the vocation that had been given to him. He also had a strong devotion to the Mother of God, and the prospect of visiting the many shrines dedicated to her had a great appeal to him.

In the afternoon, the pilgrims marched from the Metropolitan Hotel, where many had stayed, to Pier No. 50 North River, and there boarded the *Pereire*. A special compartment on the vessel had been fitted up for use as a chapel for the pilgrims. Nelson Baker had no fears of what might be encountered in the Old World. As he stood at the rail and watched New York City fade into the distance, he could never have imagined what he would find there — that tremendous devotion to Our Lady of Victory, which was so to influence his life and his immeasurable work for God and His Church. He had always had great devotion to the Mother of God, but it was to be multiplied many times over within the next few weeks.

Spirituality was the motif of the pilgrimage. Mass was celebrated for the pilgrims each morning, weather permitting. At 11:30 a.m., there was a novena, followed by the *Angelus*. Then at 2:30 p.m. they said the Rosary together, which was followed by a short instruction from Bishop Joseph Dwenger, C.PP.S., of Fort Wayne, Indiana, the spiritual leader of the pilgrimage. In the evening, meditation and night prayers closed their devotions.

Nelson Baker had no difficulty in becoming acquainted with the other members of the pilgrimage. Throughout his life he had the ability to attract others, and to be what might be called a "good listener." One of his associates, in later years, said that when you talked to Father Baker about a problem you felt that it became his own, and that all his prayers and all his energies would be devoted to solving the difficulty. This was not through any promises that he made, but rather through his deep personal interest in all those who approached him.

As they talked about the famous shrines they were to visit, Nelson Baker became intrigued with one in particular — Our Lady of Victory in Paris. Bishop Dwenger told him about it: "We all have devotion to our Lady, but I have a particular devotion to her under the title of Our Lady of Victory. My brother was suffering from an illness that seemed incurable, and we feel that he was cured through her intercession. And so, while I am delighted to go to our Lady's shrine at Lourdes, and to see the Holy Father in Rome, I particularly want to say thanks to our Lady in her church in Paris — at Our Lady of Victory." Nelson Baker felt a sudden attraction to Our Lady of Victory, and he too determined to visit her shrine.

Another pilgrim who attracted his particular attention was a Father Meulder, who had worked among the Negroes in Louisville, Kentucky. "They're a wonderful people," he told Mr. Baker. "Faithful and devoted to the Church. But they have suffered so much!"

"I know," said Nelson Baker. "I was on guard duty in New York City during the draft riots in the Civil War, and they were shamefully treated."

Father Meulder nodded his agreement. "I have a friend who was with the navy for a few years. He would often tell me of their ships chasing a 'slaver' loaded with Negroes from

45

Africa. When the navy ship began to get close, they would throw the Negroes overboard, just to lighten the cargo and to aid their own escape."

The priest was partially paralyzed but had nevertheless undertaken the voyage. He struggled to his feet, as Nelson Baker helped him. "Here, let me show you what they're sending to the Holy Father." In his cabin, he showed a gold-knobbed cane which his Negro parishioners were sending the Pope, with an address to be read, as well as a silver crown to be given to Our Lady of Lourdes, and a golden heart to be placed in the shrine of the Sacred Heart at Paray-le-Monial.

"They are not wealthy people, of course," Father Meulder continued, "but generous almost to a fault, once they know you are interested in them. If you ever get a chance to help the Negroes, Mr. Baker, I hope you will seize it. You may bring countless souls to heaven, and you will find them most willing workers for the Faith."

Nelson Baker remembered; and though he did not know it then, the time would come when, with his great spirit of charity, he would be able to help thousands of Negroes in their bitter hour of need.

The pilgrimage was not all spirituality, however. Some of the ship's crew, with a malicious sense of the penitent way of pilgrims, decided to encourage that spirit, and put hard peas into the pilgrims' shoes, left outside the cabin doors for shining.

One of the pilgrims rushed up to Nelson Baker the next morning and cried, "Look!" As he turned a shoe upside down, a handful of peas dropped to the deck.

"I know," said Nelson. "I found some in mine."

"Aren't you going to complain? To think of putting these hard peas in our shoes!"

Nelson laughed at the man's seriousness. Then he said, "If this is all the discomfort we encounter, we have little cause to complain. Think how much worse it would have been if the peas were boiled — a soft, squishy mess to clean out of

46

your shoes! This is just a little thing, a minor discomfort, lest we become too comfortable in our placid pilgrimage."

The voyage was uneventful. The *Pereire* arrived at Brest at noon on Tuesday, May 26. The pilgrims landed at Havre on the 27th and then proceeded to Paris.

There they were received by Cardinal Guibert, the Archbishop of Paris, and by his invitation attended Mass in his private chapel on May 29 and received Communion from his hands. Nelson Baker was impressed by the welcome from the Cardinal and by his interest in the Americans.

"I envy you," said the Cardinal. "You are now on your way to Rome to visit our dear Holy Father in order that, by your prayers and manifestations of your love and devotion, you may console him in his present affliction. Our Holy Mother the Church is today passing through a persecution which, though perchance surpassed heretofore in violence and animosity, is nevertheless undoubtedly more dangerous in its effects. Before the world was arrayed openly against the Church; today the world pretends to ignore but secretly and in an underhanded manner seeks to undermine and destroy her; for the society of our day is not Christian, not founded on true principles."

The pilgrims had not intended to stay very long in Paris. However, the Central Bureau of Pilgrimages advised them that there were so many pilgrims at Lourdes for May 30 and 31 that they could not possibly find accommodations. Therefore, they remained in Paris until Monday, the first of June.

Nelson Baker considered this delay a providential one. He had managed a quick visit to the shrine of Our Lady of Victory, but now, with the extra time at their disposal, Bishop Dwenger arranged to say Mass at the celebrated shrine. Nelson Baker seemed lost in thought as he looked about the church, the physical evidences of cures achieved through the intercession of Our Lady of Victory, and it seemed to him, too, that Our Lady of Victory had a special message for him.

At the conclusion of the Mass, Bishop Dwenger paid public tribute to Our Lady of Victory, then gave each pilgrim "The Cross of Pilgrimages," which had been blessed by Pope Pius IX for this special intention. Nelson Baker advanced slowly with the others and knelt at the Communion rail, to receive this "Red Cross" from Bishop Dwenger, which he then fastened on his coat.

After Paris came Lourdes. The trip was a hard and rugged one, some twenty hours by train from Paris, when they arrived in the shabby railroad station in the quaint little town at 8:55 a.m. on June 2. Everyone was tired, but most of them — as did Nelson Baker — went at once to the grotto to visit the shrine.

The church was beautiful, but Nelson hurried to the grotto itself, where our Lady had appeared to little Bernadette. As he knelt there, he saw the niche where our Lady had appeared, a perfect oval, just wide and high enough to hold a tall human figure. He saw the same type tree struggling about the rock where our Lady had stood, and it was almost as though he too could see her there.

The statue of our Lady, as described by Bernadette, stood in the niche. Nelson was filled with a prayer of thankfulness, as he recalled the many gifts he had received from God through His Blessed Mother — his vocation to the priesthood, his recovery from that serious illness, his opportunity to make this first American pilgrimage. Here, too, he saw the crutches, canes, the wooden shapes of arms, hands, and legs, the iron leggings — all the mementoes left by those who had been cured.

At Lourdes the pilgrims left the beautifully inscribed banner which they had brought from the United States. It hung with the other banners in the church, and helped them form its only decoration. They hung from the ceiling and around the walls, producing an impression of great richness and splendor.

The pilgrims left Lourdes on June 5 for Marseilles, and

then took a steamer for Civitavecchia, where the railroad took them to Rome. Shortly after their arrival, they had the long-awaited audience with the Holy Father, Pope Pius IX.

It was an emotion-filled time for all of them, as they patiently awaited the moment of their audience with the aging Supreme Pontiff. They had been told that the Pope was growing weaker day by day, and it was rumored, also, that several representatives of foreign governments had notified their governments to that effect, which added to their own concern.

But at last the time came, and they were welcomed with special fervor by the Holy Father. Bishop Dwenger spoke in the name of all the pilgrims, as he assured Pius IX of the unalterable devotion of Catholics of the United States to the Supreme Pontiff. As Americans, strongly loving liberty, the Fort Wayne Bishop said, they strongly condemned the tyrannical oppression of the Church.

Then the Holy Father replied to Bishop Dwenger's remarks: "May God bless you, dear souls, and turn His regards upon you and your country — a young country, and a young and vigorous nation, in which the products of nature and industry flourish admirably, and where the Catholic religion enjoys unlimited liberty. There true believers multiply, and so many conversions have influenced the establishment of a great number of new dioceses. . . . May it please the Lord to give the light of His truth to so many millions of souls, to the end that they also may enjoy the fruit of divine redemption."

The American pilgrims advanced, one by one, kissed the Holy Father's hand, and presented to him the gifts which they had brought from the United States. Nelson Baker's hand trembled a bit as he presented the scroll and the monetary offering from Our Lady of the Angels Seminary, and he remembered with a joyous gratitude and a full heart ever after the gracious smile of the Holy Father as he received the gifts.

On Thursday, July 11, the Holy Father celebrated Mass especially for the Americans, and Nelson Baker, with the rest of the pilgrims, had the unusual privilege of receiving Communion from the hands of Pope Pius IX.

The pilgrimage had officially ended with their reception by the Supreme Pontiff, but many of the pilgrims remained several days longer in Rome. Nelson Baker was one of those who remained to participate in the celebration of the Pope's twenty-eighth anniversary on June 20. He spent some time visiting the churches and holy places of Rome, his thoughts often with the martyrs who had walked those same streets in bygone years.

It was on one of these excursions that he heard an English voice shouting, "Long live the Pope!" and then an excited clamor in Italian. He hurried around a street corner, and saw two English tourists or pilgrims surrounded by Italian police, with onlookers crowding about them. It seemed as though the pilgrims were being arrested, and he tried to push his slight frame through the mass of people that had gathered. He was about to add his protest to theirs, when he felt a gentle hand on his shoulder.

"Come this way, my friend," a quiet voice said, and as he turned, he saw a bewhiskered priest beckoning him aside.

"You will accomplish nothing by barging in," the priest said in English. "I know. You will end by being carted off to jail, as they will be."

"But can they be arrested merely for saying, 'Long live the Pope'?"

The elderly priest smiled. "They not only can be, but they are. Some of the Italians are very nationalistic right now. There is much antagonism by some people in authority against the Holy Father."

"But we can't let this happen!"

"We must. If we protest — and I admit I feel as you do — we too will go off to jail, and nothing is accomplished. If we go to the English embassy, they will see that our imprudent pilgrims are promptly released, none the worse for their adventure."

Nelson still hesitated, but the priest took him by the arm and walked down the street with him. "We are guests here in Italy," he said. "Feelings run high, at this time, and it is not wise to rouse the tempers of our hosts when there is no need to do so." As Nelson walked farther toward the embassy, he began to realize the wisdom of the priest's advice, and willingly continued with him.

Soon afterward he started on his journey back home, going by way of Loretto, where he visited the Holy House of Nazareth, and the shrine at Paray-le-Monial in the Convent of the Visitation, where our Lord appeared to St. Margaret Mary Alacoque (then Blessed Margaret Mary), and from which has grown the special devotion to our Savior on the First Fridays.

He stopped again in Paris, where he spent much time at Notre Dame des Victoires, gazing at the lovely figure of Our Lady of Victory with her divine Son. There, too, he promised that when the opportunity came, he would do all he could to further devotion to our Lady under that special title.

Nelson Baker sailed from Havre, France, early in July, and arrived in New York City on July 14, 1874, one of the first of the American pilgrims to return home.

CHAPTER **VII**

SOON he was back at work at the seminary, where he continued to receive high marks and awards for his fine work. One of his classmates recalled that "in study hall days, a familiar sight was Nelson Baker taking his constitutional, a trot around the walk between rising time and time for morning prayers and Mass. He was always abstemious, a graham cracker would suffice him."

He progressed rapidly in the seminary, and on December 18, 1875, he received minor orders and tonsure from his friend, Bishop Ryan. Then, on March 11, 1876, he was raised to the diaconate. A few days later, he was called to the rector's office, where he found two fellow seminarians.

"The Bishop would like to see you three gentlemen at three o'clock tomorrow afternoon," the rector said. The three shot worried glances at each other.

"Oh, it's nothing to worry about. I suspect the Bishop wants to ordain you before the rest of the class, because the need for priests in the Buffalo diocese is so great. We are a bit sorry, because we would like to have you ordained here. But the need for priests is immediate, and I suspect the Bishop has no choice."

The Bishop confirmed the rector's suggestion, and told the young men that they would be ordained on March 19 in St. Joseph's Cathedral, Buffalo. "I know the seminary would prefer to have you ordained with your class, and so would I, in ordinary circumstances. But we have a great need for priests, and I have decided to ordain you now. I have watched your work at the seminary. I am sure you will devote yourselves wholeheartedly to your great calling in the priesthood of our Lord."

Four priests for the Buffalo diocese were ordained on that feast of St. Joseph in 1876 — Nelson H. Baker, John C. Long, Maurice J. Lee, and James P. Lasher. Father Baker was then 34 years old, and entering into the lifework he had sought so long.

Tears filled his mother's eyes as she knelt for his first blessing; and his father and brothers were well impressed by Nelson's accomplishment. They had not been enthusiastic about his studying for the priesthood, but if he wanted it, as certainly he did, it was all right with them.

That afternoon, Lewis Baker's practical mind asked a question many of them had wondered about. "What happens now, Nelson? What do you do now?"

"It all depends on the Bishop," Father Baker replied. "He will decide where I'll be stationed. It might be here in Buffalo, or somewhere else in the diocese — wherever he decides that I'm needed."

"Don't you have anything to say about it?"

Father Baker laughed. "Not really. Of course, if there were a good reason for not being assigned to a certain place, the Bishop would listen to your comment. But he is the one who decides. I'm going to be at the seminary for a few days, and I'll say my first Mass there on March 22. It would make me very happy if you could all be there."

"Of course, Nelson," said his mother quickly. "We'll all be there." His father spoke more slowly, but he too agreed. "Of course. We'll be most happy to come."

When, a few days later, Father Baker called on Bishop Ryan to receive his appointment, he found to his astonishment that he was to be assistant superintendent of the institutions at Limestone Hill, under Father Hines. "I realize," said the

Bishop, "that this is an unusual assignment for a newly ordained priest. But you have a good business background, you are older, and I am sure you will be very helpful to Father Hines."

"I'll do the best I can," said Father Baker earnestly.

"I'm sure you will. I've watched your work with the boys at the seminary, and I think you have a natural knack for getting the best out of them."

Father Hines welcomed his new assistant with open arms, and Father Baker plunged into the work. The financial situation at the institutions was desperate, as Father Hines told him one day. They were sitting in Father Hines's office when Father Baker noticed how tired he looked. "You should get more rest, Father," he said. "You'll wear yourself out."

Father Hines shook his head wearily. "It isn't the work, Father Baker. It's the worry. Right now St. John's Protectory owes $19,000 — and we've got only $100. St. Joseph's Orphan Asylum owes nearly $8,000 — and we have less than $100 in cash there."

"How do you manage? Many of these children are wards of the state. Doesn't the state provide enough for their care?"

"Not nearly enough," said Father Hines with a wry smile. "Not nearly enough. If it were not for the heroic work of the Sisters of St. Joseph at the orphan asylum, and the Brothers of the Holy Infancy at the Protectory, we couldn't have existed this long. It is a constant struggle. But we do our best — and God will provide."

There was great need in those days for institutions such as St. Joseph's Boys Orphan Asylum and St. John's Protectory. The number of boys at each institution increased year by year — and so, unfortunately, did the debt which the institutions carried. By 1881, the amount owed by St. John's Protectory had jumped to over $56,000 — a tremendous sum of money in those days.

In that same year, Father Baker was transferred from the charitable institutions at Limestone Hill, in the town of West

Seneca, to St. Mary's parish, Corning, New York, which was then a part of the Buffalo diocese.

Brother Stanislaus, of the Brothers of the Holy Infancy, who spent thirty-two years at the institutions with Father Baker, says that "Father Baker asked the Bishop to change him because, he told me, he didn't see any hope for this place. It was doomed to failure, to close up."

Father Baker was not to stay long at the Corning parish, just about a year, but even in that short time, from approximately February, 1881, to February, 1882, he made quite an impression on the people of the parish and on the town of Corning itself. Father Robert F. McNamara, in his history of the parish, *A Century of Grace*, wrote that Father Baker "had endeared himself to the parishioners for his earnestness and piety, and even for his alleged ability to work miracles."

Referring to these "miracles," Father McNamara wrote: "Three of these alleged cures can be mentioned here. When the writer's aunt Kate Dwyer recovered from typhoid fever after Father Baker had prayed over her and applied Lourdes water, it was firmly believed that his intervention was responsible for the cure.

"Frank Walker's recovery from diphtheria was likewise attributed to the efficacy of Father Baker's prayers.

"Mrs. William Killigrew tells me that her father, Dennis McCarty of Caton, was convinced that he owed his cure of a painful kidney ailment to the same priest's intercession. Father Baker came out to visit the sick man, took a glass of water, stirred it with his fingers and gave it to him to drink, saying, 'You will be all right.' The priest had only reached the bottom of the hill on his return journey when Mr. McCarty's pain ceased and never thereafter did it return. . . ."

Brother Stanislaus also refers to these same words, "You will be all right," in talking about Father Baker. "One thing about him — if he would go to see a person who was very sick and would say, 'Now, you are going to be all right,' the patient recovered. If he said, 'Whatever our Lord wills,' then

55

the patient wouldn't recover. He didn't always die. But any time Father Baker said, 'You are going to be all right,' the patient recovered."

In that February of 1882, a message came to Father Baker that Bishop Ryan wanted to see him, and so he went back to Buffalo. Father Baker was now forty years old, even though he had been a priest only six years.

The Bishop came quickly to the point. "Father, I'd like you to go to Limestone Hill to take Father Hines's place. He is moving to a parish where the work will be less strenuous."

"But, Bishop," said Father Baker, "I don't feel qualified for the work. You need a more capable man, a more experienced priest."

The Bishop smiled at Father Baker's protests. "You are too modest, Father. I've talked this over with Father Hines, and he thinks you are just the man for the position. And I think so too."

Father Baker thoughtfully pulled at his nose, and then said, "I don't like to disagree with you, Bishop, but honestly, I don't feel I'm the man for Limestone Hill."

"Since you feel so strongly about it, Father, let's both think it over until tomorrow. You say your Mass for the right decision, and so will I; and then come to see me again."

The next morning Father Baker felt the same way. "I'm sorry, Bishop, but I feel just as I did yesterday."

Again the Bishop smiled. "And so do I, Father. So go out to Limestone Hill and do the best you can. As you know from your own work there, many difficulties must be faced — and I think you're the only one who can solve them. God be with you."

At Limestone Hill, Father Baker was pastor of St. Patrick's Church and superintendent of both St. John's Protectory and St. Joseph's Orphan Asylum, with all these people dependent upon him. He had been in full charge for only a few days when a group of creditors came to call on him.

"We need our money," one said bluntly. "We don't know you, Father. We knew Father Hines, and perhaps we let things go too long — but we need our money, and we need it now."

Father Baker looked over the six or seven men gathered in the room and asked very calmly, "Do all of you feel the same way?"

Most of them said "Yes," but one man stood up and said, "I think I know you. Aren't you the Baker of Meyer and Baker, feed and grain, that used to be down on Washington Street?"

"Yes," said Father Baker. "I used to do business with you then."

"I thought so," said the man. "Your word is good enough for me, Father. If you can assure me that I'll be paid reasonably soon, I'll go along for anything you want."

"Thank you," Father Baker replied. "The rest of you bring your accounts here in the morning. I'll pay them in full. But don't come back seeking any more business from these institutions. Thank you, gentlemen." And he began to walk away.

"Wait! Wait!" the other men shouted.

Father Baker turned and faced them. "Gentlemen, business is built on mutual trust. If you don't trust me, I don't see why I should trust you. But . . . if you want to reconsider, you may discuss that with me in the morning." And he walked out of the room.

Getting into his buggy, he drove down to Buffalo that afternoon and drew out all the savings accumulated during his business career, so that the money would be available to pay off the bills of the institutions and the boys would not go hungry. Some creditors insisted on being paid in full, but only a few; the others were willing to receive part of their bill and wait for the rest.

The situation, however, was critical. Father Baker knew that some way had to be found to secure more money. The parish was small and he could expect little from the people.

57

One night, as he knelt in St. Patrick's Church, his mind turned back to the days in Paris, and to Our Lady of Victory. He remembered her silent promise to help him in his work — and then he got the idea for an Association of Our Lady of Victory.

He formed the Association and then began to let people know about it. Each night, after his heavy day's work had been done, he sat at the rolltop desk in his office, and wrote letters to postmasters all over the United States. Would they send him the names of a few Catholic women in their city, who might assist this work for dependent and helpless boys? Night after night, he wrote the letters, and soon the replies began to come back.

Then the second stage began, writing letters to these Catholic ladies, asking their assistance. Would they join the Association of Our Lady of Victory? Would they ask friends to join? The cost was slight, only twenty-five cents a year. His letters began to bring results, and soon it was no longer possible to write the letters himself. Father Baker began his first publication, which he called *Appeal for the Homeless and Destitute Children.*

Through this publication, he told of the work he was trying to do and of the great danger to the faith of orphaned Catholic children. In the larger cities, children would lose their parents in epidemics and be homeless, wandering about the streets. "Sending Societies" were organized, which gathered up the children, put them into secular institutions, and then sent them to the Middle West, to live with farm families.

In one of the early issues, Father Baker wrote of the societies "which have been engaged for years in entrapping by one means or another our little Irish children and giving them into homes of non-Catholic farmers where they are lost forever to the Faith."

To help save the faith of these children, he opened the doors of his institutions to them. And he appealed to the Catholic people of the country to help him. They did help;

their response made it possible for him to erect more buildings and to help many more children.

Members of the Association received many spiritual benefits, among them seven novenas of Masses offered at the Limestone Hill institutions, and 100 Masses offered at each of seven remarkable shrines: Our Lady of Victory in Paris, Our Lady of Lourdes, Our Lady of Loretto, Our Lady of Perpetual Help in Rome, Our Lady of Mt. Carmel in Rome, Our Lady of Knock in Ireland, and the Shrine of the Sacred Heart of Jesus, Paray-le-Monial, France.

As members of the Association responded to Father Baker's pleas, he began his first building project, an addition to St. John's Protectory, so that he could care for more boys. In this he built a beautiful chapel, with a statue of Our Lady of Victory, imported from France.

For years this chapel was used for the boys in the Protectory. Father Baker said Mass for them there every morning. After Mass he would talk to them, and visitors to St. John's Protectory were sometimes surprised (and perhaps even shocked) to hear three cheers for our Lady coming from the chapel. But Father Baker had his own way of spreading devotion to Our Lady of Victory, and it worked for him!

After Mass, too, the boys would pray for the Brothers and the Sisters who had died at their institutions. On one side a large plaque had the names of all the Sisters who had died; on the other side, the names of the Brothers who had died. Father Baker would call for prayers "for the Sisters on the wall" and "for the Brothers on the wall."

Each evening, he celebrated Benediction for his boys. They would come in from the playground in back of the Protectory, loaded down with their baseball bats and gloves and balls, so that when Benediction was over they could go out and play some more.

The new chapel and the enlarged building were dedicated on June 26, 1889, but Father Baker did not rest there.

CHAPTER VIII

FOR some years Father Baker had been watching with increasing interest the development of natural gas in the Buffalo area. Not too many years before, natural gas had been used commercially for the first time. Some had been found within the Buffalo city limits, and in 1883 the Buffalo Cement Company had gotten a small flow of gas from one well. Then in December, 1890, natural gas from the Canadian wells was turned on for the Buffalo pipelines and used to illuminate the Niagara River.

One night, as he sat in his small office, totaling up the bills for heating and lighting his institutions, Father Baker had an inspiration. What if he should drill for natural gas? A gas well would solve all his heating and lighting problems. He would have no more costly bills to pay for that purpose, and the money could be used for other needs.

Father Baker knew that he could not afford to have the natural gas piped to the institution buildings from the Canadian wells. That would be entirely too expensive. But might there be natural gas on Limestone Hill?

Methodically, he considered the arguments for and against the plan. He remembered that an expert had declared in a recent interview with the Buffalo newspapers that the supply of natural gas in the area was very limited.

Frankly, too, he told himself that he did not have enough money to drill for gas. The drillers would have to be brought from the Pennsylvania oil fields, and they would have to be paid. Drilling was an expensive business, Father Baker knew. And so now he had two questions: Was there natural gas on Limestone Hill? and Could he find the money to drill for it?

As he so often did with difficult problems, Father Baker put this one in the hands of Our Lady of Victory. Late that night he climbed the stairs to the chapel and knelt in prayer before the statue he had brought from France. He told our Lady of the great need for natural gas to aid the institutions — her institutions, he reminded her — and to help in the better care of her children.

He prayed through most of the night and then, with a characteristic pat on our Lady's cheek, he said, "Now — there it is. You take care of it, dear Lady of Victory." And off he went for a few hours of sleep, content that the problem was in the proper hands.

Each day Father Baker would walk along a path in an empty lot across from the Protectory, reading his office. "Father Baker's prayer path," some people called it, because they would often see him there, reading from his breviary and saying his prayers. And each day he remembered his gas-well project, and asked our Lady's help with it. Finally, one day, he got what he felt was his answer. A visiting priest told him that the Bishop had just received a donation of $5,000 from a friend of the diocese.

"That's wonderful!" said Father Baker. "And what is it to be used for?"

"That's the best part of it," his friend replied. "The Bishop can use it any way he wishes. There are no strings attached to the gift."

After the priest had left, Father Baker thought long and hard about the Bishop's gift. Five thousand dollars would pay for a lot of drilling. The more Father Baker thought, the more convinced he was that this was Our Lady of Victory's answer to his prayers.

But would the Bishop think so? Father Baker prayed almost

all night before the statue of Our Lady of Victory in the Protectory chapel; the next morning he was on his way into Buffalo in his buggy to see the Bishop.

After some small talk, Father Baker began to refer to his heating problems at the institutions. "Our heating bills are growing all the time, Bishop. I'd like very much to reduce them."

The Bishop smiled. "So would all of us, Father, but there's not much we can do about that."

"Yes, there is," said Father Baker. "You've read, of course, about the natural gas wells that have been drilled — "

"You're not thinking of drilling for gas, are you, Father Baker?" The Bishop's amazement showed in his voice.

"Why not?"

"Surely you're joking, Father. Just the other day some experts said there is but little natural gas in this area, and what there is will not last long. There's no evidence of any at Limestone Hill — certainly no one else has thought of drilling there." The Bishop looked at Father Baker very seriously. "You must be joking, Father."

"No, Bishop," said Father Baker very earnestly. "I have considered this very carefully. For many nights I have been praying to Our Lady of Victory for a sign and I believe that sign has been given to me. And I firmly believe that we will find natural gas when we drill in Limestone Hill."

"But there is no gas there. At least, there is no indication of it. This is visionary and impractical."

"Visionary, yes; but impractical?" Father Baker asked. "Not to Our Lady of Victory. She will see that we find it. Has Our Lady of Victory ever failed to help us, Bishop?"

Father Baker leaned back in his chair and watched the Bishop's face as he struggled with the decision. Finally, the Bishop smiled and said, "Well, Father, I cannot go against Our Lady of Victory."

"Thank you, Bishop. Now there is just one small matter. The money for the drilling. Of course we have none — "

62

"And you've heard of the $5,000 given to me? Of course, Father, I'll be happy to give you $500 for the drilling."

Father Baker shook his head stubbornly. "Such a small sum would just be thrown away, Bishop. If Our Lady of Victory is to find gas for us, can we not give her the tools to do so?"

"How much would that be?"

"At least $2,000. There is no use starting this at all unless we give our Lady a proper chance to find the gas for us. We too have to show our faith in her." Father Baker laughed ruefully. "Sometimes it seems that she deliberately tests our faith by letting us wait for success, but she never fails us."

Finally the Bishop agreed. "All right, Father Baker. You may have the $2,000 for this experiment. I only hope that you have interpreted our Lady's wishes rightly. If there is no gas, not only is the money gone, but faith in Our Lady of Victory may be lost."

Father Baker quickly got to work. In a short time drillers from the Pennsylvania oil fields pulled up in front of St. John's Protectory. The big foreman stamped into Father Baker's office, to ask where the well should be drilled.

Father Baker smiled and said, "We haven't decided yet as to the exact spot, but it will be in that field across the road. We'll know this afternoon."

"Your engineer or geologist will be here then?"

Father Baker laughed heartily. "She's not an engineer or geologist — but she knows more than any of them. She is really an expert."

The drill foreman scratched his head, mystified. "I don't know what you mean, Father. She? A woman engineer?"

Father Baker laughed again as he leaned back in his chair. "Oh, no! Our Lady of Victory, who will help us find the gas!"

"I hope you know what you're doing, Father. But what does our Lady know about gas wells?"

"Just wait, and you'll see," said Father Baker. "This afternoon, about four o'clock, I'll show you where to drill."

That afternoon the drillers were amazed to see a religious procession come out of St. Patrick's Church, with scores of altar boys, the Sisters of St. Joseph, the Brothers of the Holy Infancy, and then Father Baker. They were reciting the Rosary as they marched across the street to the vacant lot where the drilling equipment had been unloaded.

The procession sang a hymn in honor of Our Lady of Victory, and then Father Baker went to one end of the "prayer path." Solemnly he blessed the ground and sprinkled it with holy water, imploring the aid of Our Lady of Victory. Then he took a small lead statue from his pocket and buried it about a foot into the ground.

"There!" he told the drill foreman. "That's the place to put down your drill — as close to the statue as you can, but don't touch it!"

The procession re-formed and went back to the church, where Father Baker prayed again for a successful gas well for Our Lady of Victory's children who were in his care.

The drillers watched in astonishment, and one voiced his doubt. "That's supposed to tell us where to find gas?"

Soon they got to work, setting up the tower, and the hole was sunk deeper and deeper into the ground, bringing back core after core of rock and dirt, but showing no evidence of the structure where gas might be found.

Each day Father Baker visited the drilling, talking with the foreman and the drillers, never seeming concerned that there was as yet no evidence of gas.

One day the foreman said, "We're down over 600 feet now, Father. If there's gas here, we should have found it by now, or some trace of it. Do you want to keep on?"

"Of course, Tom," Father Baker replied.

"The men are grumbling a bit."

"Grumbling? Why? They're getting paid regularly. What difference does it make to them if they work here on Limestone Hill or in the Pennsylvania fields?"

"It isn't that, Father," said the foreman. "But they hate

64

to see all this money going into a dry hole, when it might be doing something for the kids in the orphans' home or in the Protectory."

Father Baker's face was serious. "I appreciate how they feel, Tom, believe me. I have the responsibility of caring for these children. If I'm wasting money that belongs to them, I'll have to answer for it. But Our Lady of Victory has a greater responsibility than all of us. This work is dedicated to her. I've called our work here 'Our Lady of Victory's Care.' She wouldn't let us go wrong. So keep drilling. And when we've shown sufficient faith, Our Lady of Victory will provide gas for us."

The $2,000 provided by the Bishop was soon gone, and Father Baker had to go back to him again for more funds, until eventually he had been given the entire $5,000.

The well went down deeper, eight hundred, nine hundred, even a thousand feet. Only a few people watched the drilling now — "Father Baker's Folly," they called it. July went past, and then came August, with the annual novena in honor of the Assumption of our Lady.

People thought perhaps on that great feast day of our Lady some signs of success would come — but they didn't. The novena went on day by day, and prayers by the thousands ascended into heaven. And the drill went deeper and deeper into the earth, with no results.

After the novena in honor of the Assumption, Father Baker started another novena for the specific purpose of striking gas. Again the prayers rose to heaven, and for eight days the drill went deeper and deeper.

On the evening of the eighth day, on August 21, 1891, Father Baker was celebrating Benediction in St. Patrick's Church. He had not quite finished when a messenger hurried into the church and hesitantly approached.

"Father!" he whispered. "They think they've struck gas. They want you at the well!"

Father Baker nodded to show that he had heard and continued his prayers. Then he added a few others in thanksgiving before he went to the drilling site. Some people in the church, who had heard the message, were impatient to hurry over there, but they waited until Father Baker had finished.

When the drill foreman saw Father Baker coming, he ran toward him. "We've struck it, Father! Your Lady of Victory was right!"

One of the drillers, called the Wild Irishman, came up and said, "Don't get your hopes up too high, Father. The gas hasn't come in yet." He shook his head mournfully. "You can never tell."

The foreman showed Father Baker a drill core of sand. "This is the type sand that usually contains gas, and we've just come into it."

Father Baker smiled. "That looks good, Tom. What do we do now?"

"We keep drilling, and see if we really do strike gas, and just how much. The Wild Irishman is right in a way. It might be just a little pocket that doesn't amount to much. But this is the first sign we've had and to me it looks real good."

"Our Lady of Victory promised, Tom, and she always does what she promises." Father Baker pulled out his watch. "It's pretty late now. Let's stop till the morning."

That night Father Baker knelt before our Lady's statue in the Protectory chapel to thank her for the good indications that had come from the drilling and to pray that gas in good supply would come. As he knelt there, he remembered the many difficulties that had to be overcome: the drill bits that had broken on hard rock, the tools lost down the hole and then "fished out," and he was more grateful than ever that success at last seemed to be in sight.

Word had spread through West Seneca, as Limestone Hill was now called, and hundreds of people gathered around the drilling rig. The date was August 22, 1891. Years later that date would be dedicated to the Immaculate Heart of Mary.

The drilling started, and after two feet, at a total depth

66

of 1137 feet, the foreman turned a stream of water into the hole. The pressure of the gas shot it back up in a spray.

"We've got it! We've got it!" he cried, and Father Baker's wide smile showed his quiet satisfaction.

But the Wild Irishman still doubted it. "It's just a pocket," he growled. "I could hold it down myself!" He put a large pail over the well and sat on it, to see if he could hold down the gas. He couldn't. The gas pushed up against the pail, swirled and whirled under it, and finally blew the Wild Irishman to one side, shooting out in every direction.

Unfortunately, it reached the fire in a nearby forge, used to sharpen the tools. There was a terrible explosion as the gas caught fire. The flames shot eighty feet into the air, and were blazing eight feet across as the gas roared out of the drill hole. Five men were badly burned as they tried to save the tools and the derrick, and three small boys were burned as they got too near the fire.

The gas blazed all through the day, shooting high up into the sky and attracting people from all over the area. It burned until three o'clock in the afternoon, when the drillers shot a heavy stream of water across the hole to cut off the air from the gas, and then plugged the hole with a heavy timber.

Father Baker immediately telegraphed Bishop Ryan, telling him of the discovery of gas. Soon the Bishop came out in his buggy to see the Victoria Well, as Father Baker had named it. When he saw the charred timbers and the burned area around the well, he asked, "What's happened, Father?"

Father Baker explained about the explosion and fire, and the people who had been burned. "But they will recover, Bishop, I'm sure. The doctors are caring for them, and they are resting as comfortably as they can."

"Give them my blessings too when you call on them, Father," said the Bishop. "And congratulations to you on this fine well — and on your perseverance."

"Not to me, Bishop," said Father Baker, "but to Our Lady of Victory."

67

CHAPTER IX

THE well caused a sensation in Buffalo as well as at Limestone Hill. Speculators circulated among the farmers, signing
up properties for leases as they tried to find gas in the area.
Numerous wells were drilled, but generally with little success. Father Baker's was the first well drilled in the West
Seneca area; he was, as one oil expert said, "the great pioneer
in this business."

The newspapers were filled with rumors and gossip about
the Victoria Well, one story stating that Father Baker had
been offered the tremendous sum of $60,000 for a lease of
200 acres of Protectory property. According to a reporter,
this story "was placed point blank before Father Baker. The
only answer was a significant smile. He said the well had
not been sold."

Some of the people drilling for gas in West Seneca were
unscrupulous in their efforts to tap the same pool as the
Victoria Well. One syndicate drilled a short distance from
Father Baker's well, as one report stated, "with the hope of
striking the same vein of gas and selling out to the Standard
Oil Company which has a pipeline laid a few hundred feet
away. The people generally deplored the attempt to destroy
the value of the Victoria Well.

"The work . . . was getting on swimmingly and a depth
of 600 feet had been reached. This morning about daylight
. . . the contractor discovered that something was wrong, and

with a strong suspicion of what had happened, he pulled the string of tools to the surface, and found the big stem, 30 feet long, badly twisted. A flinty boulder had been struck and the hole at a considerable depth had veered over five feet out of line, making it next to impossible to continue drilling. The bent stem has been sent to Buffalo to be straightened. Experts say that it will hardly be possible to break the 'hardhead' that switched the tools out of plumb after $1,200 had been spent in drilling, and it looks as though the hole must be abandoned. No closer location to the Victoria Well can be obtained except upon the lands of the Rt. Rev. Bishop Ryan."

Some experts have felt that Father Baker's gas well may have hit a pool by itself, because there have been dry holes drilled all around it.

The Victoria Well provided plenty of gas to heat the buildings, to provide light for them, and to do the cooking that was needed. In fact, Father Baker had so much gas that he brought in a carload of pipes to deliver the gas to all who wished to burn it, within two miles of the well. The charge was a most moderate one, "not to exceed $15 a year per stove."

It was estimated that the gas well saved Father Baker $3,000 a year in fuel, and it also furnished fifty families with heat and light. However, Father Baker did not continue to supply natural gas to all the homes in the vicinity. After a while, the pressure in the well began to drop and, many people believe, he concluded that Our Lady of Victory intended the gas well to supply only the institutions and not the whole town of West Seneca. At any rate, he discontinued supplying gas outside the institutions.

Some years later, when the first well was closed down for repairs, Father Baker decided it was uneconomical to buy fuel to heat the institutions during that period. Therefore, he had another well drilled a short distance away, and this too came in. Since then the institutions of Our Lady of Victory have never had to purchase gas.

As this is written sixty-eight years later, Victoria Well still supplies ample gas for Our Lady of Victory institutions. For some years, the gas has only been used for cooking purposes, but this includes the large hospital, the infant home, the nurses' home, and all the other related activities of Our Lady of Victory's Homes of Charity, which comprise a small city in themselves.

Father Baker was not free from concern and worry even after the first well came in so fully. He was concerned especially about the three small boys who had been burned in the explosion. One of them, Eddie Sours, had been blown some fifty feet by the explosion, and the reports said that he was in a precarious condition and might die. His brother had been burned too, but not so badly — and Mrs. Sours was very upset when Father Baker came to call one day.

"The newspaper stories, Father," she said tearfully, "they frighten me. They say that Eddie is going to die."

"Now, now," Father Baker soothed her. "Don't worry, Mrs. Sours. Eddie is going to be all right — and so is Joe, and Fritz Walker. Don't worry. Our Lady of Victory will take care of them."

When Father Baker talked to Eddie, he told him the same — "You are going to be all right." Then he blessed Eddie and his brother, and pinned on each a medal of Our Lady of Victory.

They were all right, too. As the papers reported a few weeks later, "the recovery of the three little boys burned in the explosion has been phenomenal. Eddie Sours, who it was thought could hardly recover, is rapidly gaining strength and his face is nearly healed without any appearance of scars. His legs are healing in a satisfactory way and he will soon be able to be about."

Then, in October, another fire struck the big Victoria Well. Father Baker was on his way to the chapel when he heard the explosion and the roar of the flames. The memory of the first fire was still vivid in his mind, and he knew what had

70

happened even before he turned to look out the window by the stairs.

A solid column of blue flame shot many feet into the air, as one observer said, "twisting and turning like a monster snake." As he hurried to the well, Father Baker prayed that no one had been hurt by the fire and explosion; and fortunately no one had. He found that a careless workman had carried a lighted lamp into the shed covering the valves of the well, and that caused the explosion.

The local fire companies raced to the fire but they had no success in stopping it. Then the fire department of Buffalo was telegraphed to send help. One of the Buffalo engines came out and pumped two water wells dry, trying to stop the flames, without success. Fifty thousand feet of natural gas went up in flames every hour — and there seemed to be no prospect of stopping the fire until millions of feet of gas had been wasted. Fortunately, there was no danger to the adjoining property, though the heat from the fire was intense.

For two days and nights all efforts to stop the fire failed. Then the foreman of the chair factory at St. John's Protectory — where the boys learned that trade — came to Father Baker and said, "Father, it seems that we could pipe live steam to the well and put out the fire that way."

"I had thought of that," Father Baker admitted, "but it's pretty dangerous."

"Nothing else has worked, and some of the men are willing to try it."

Father Baker started to object, and then the foreman said, "Father, this is for Our Lady of Victory. Don't you think she'll protect us?"

Wearing heavy coats soaked with water to protect them from the heat, the men crawled close to the flaming gas and unscrewed the connecting pipes. Then other men forced live steam across the flaming crater of gas. The flames were blown away, and then came back again. Once more the men tried — and this time the fire was snuffed out! Suddenly the night was the blackest black, as all the light from the fire was gone. Someone in the distance lit an oil lamp, and then another, and by these flickering lights the well was capped to stop the flow of gas.

There was an amusing aftermath to the Victoria Well which brought so much fame and activity to Limestone Hill. The following January, Father Baker suggested that Victoria might be a good name for that particular section of West Seneca, which then took in an area as great as the city of Buffalo itself.

There was certainly considerable merit to Father Baker's suggestion. The post office at Limestone Hill did a sizable business of about $1,600 a year — a goodly amount for that time — and was among the best paying of the fourth-class post offices. Another factor was that nine tenths of the mail handled there was either from or for St. John's Protectory, for Father Baker's Association of Our Blessed Lady of Victory. Father Baker, you see, was a pioneer in many things — not only in drilling for gas wells, but in what is usually considered a relatively modern enterprise, "direct mail" promotion.

His suggestion of changing the name to Victoria, however, met with violent and heated protests. The letter columns of the daily papers bristled with indignation. One gentleman was very excited because Victoria was the name of the British queen; he felt that undue honor was being paid to her. Another objected because Victoria, New York, might be confused with another Victoria across the Canadian border. And still another wrote to the Buffalo *Evening News*, demanding: "Can nothing be done to extinguish the lawless name-fiend who delights in changing the name of some post office? I see by your columns that he is now advocating a change from West Seneca to Victoria."

The net result was that the name remained as West Seneca for many years to come. It also showed that, contrary to what some people have come to believe, Father Baker did

72

not always get his own way, and that frequently his ideas were opposed. Regardless of the public protest, Father Baker liked the name as a tribute to Our Lady of Victory and continued to use it. For many years, the title page of his magazine, *The Victorian*, carried the address of "Victoria, West Seneca, N. Y." In May, 1904, Father Baker changed this designation to "Victorhill, N. Y.," and eventually the town's name was officially changed to the present one of Lackawanna.

Several significant events marked the year of 1894. In that year, Father Baker erected a wayside shrine next to the main building of St. John's Protectory. It was, in a sense, a simple shrine, with the statue of Our Lady of Victory standing on a red-brick base and protected by a canopy. Two small pillars stood in front of it, with flowers placed on them; a curved path led up to the shrine, with a border of flowers alongside.

In 1924, when the beautiful national shrine of Our Lady of Victory was under construction, the wayside shrine was transferred across the street, where it now stands between St. Joseph's Orphanage and Our Lady of Victory Infant Home. It is a favorite with pilgrims, who stop there to pray, and often to have a friend take their picture as a souvenir of their visit to Our Lady of Victory Homes of Charity.

In that same year of 1894, a young man of 18 came from Horseheads, New York, to join the Brothers of the Holy Infancy and Youth of Jesus as Brother Stanislaus, and to become an invaluable assistant to Father Baker.

Father Baker's mother had died in 1885. After that, his father Lewis came often to visit his son at Lackawanna. During one of these visits he became ill. Mr. Baker was then 76 years old. Father Baker told Brother Stanislaus, "You had better stay with the old gentleman. He's rather sick. Be sure to call me if he gets worse."

About three o'clock in the morning, Lewis Baker did seem to be getting worse, and Brother Stanislaus hurried to Father Baker's room. "You'd better come, Father. He seems to be sinking."

Father Baker came quickly, and the old man looked up at him and said slowly, struggling for strength, "Anything that will separate me from my dead wife Caroline, son, please remove it."

Father Baker knelt by the bedside and told his father, "Nothing but Baptism." His dying father smiled and nodded his head. Quickly, Brother Stanislaus called some of the Sisters for witnesses, and Father Baker baptized Lewis Baker into his faith and the faith of his dead wife. He then anointed him, as the Sisters and Brother Stanislaus recited the prayers for the dying and for the eternal repose of his soul.

CHAPTER X

IN 1901 Father Baker celebrated his silver jubilee in the priesthood. A familiar and respected personage in the Buffalo area, he was now fifty-nine years old. One would think that he was nearing the age when many men begin to look forward to the quiet period of life, to enjoy the fruits of their labors and let younger men take over the burdens and the stresses of meeting the ever recurring daily problems and responsibilities — and, of course, Father Baker had these in great abundance.

In the wonderful providence of God, however, Father Baker's greatest achievements lay ahead of him. A stranger, seeing him walk along the streets of West Seneca, would think he had not a care in the world. Father Baker always had plenty of time to talk to passers-by and a pocketful of Our Lady of Victory medals for the children — for those adults, too, who did not have one or more already.

When anyone stopped him to talk about a problem, Father Baker gave him all his attention, his eyes intent behind the steel-rimmed glasses. Then, when the problem had been presented, he would say gently, "Now, now, Pete or Joe or Mary, everything is going to be all right. You pray to Our Lady of Victory, and I'll pray to her, too, for your intention. You'll see, everything will be all right." And if material aid were needed, Father Baker saw that it was forthcoming, quickly and quietly.

During Father Baker's time at West Seneca as superintendent of the Protectory, the number of boys in his care had increased tremendously. In 1883, the average number of boys was 120; in 1901, the average was 385. St. Joseph's Boys' Orphan Asylum had grown, too, from 118 children to 236.

A new venture had been added, the Working Boys' Home of the Sacred Heart in Buffalo, with 80 boys in residence. This was a home for the older boys who had left the Protectory and were now working in Buffalo's industries.

Members of the Association of Our Lady of Victory contributed much to the support and upkeep of the institutions at West Seneca, but Father Baker did not neglect the traditional means of parish and church fund-raising. Picnics and excursion boat rides on the lake and river brought in much needed funds.

In 1894 he had built a new structure to replace the old St. John's Protectory, and in 1897 he had added a wing to that, so that now the Protectory boys were housed and schooled in a magnificent five-story building. Father Thomas A. Galvin, C.Ss.R., who was brought up in Father Baker's homes and prided himself as being "one of Father Baker's boys," has described the building in his book, A Modern Apostle of Charity. It had a frontage of 275 feet, and its depth at the southernmost limit was 562 feet, and "to the top of the statue of Our Blessed Lady of Victory which graces the cupola it rises to a height of 160 feet." The building had a total of 190 rooms for living quarters and 30 rooms for the trades schools.

In December, 1903, the first of many ecclesiastical honors came to Father Baker. Bishop James E. Quigley had succeeded Bishop Ryan in 1897, and in 1903 he was named the Archbishop of Chicago. His successor in Buffalo was Bishop Charles H. Colton. A few months after his consecration, he named Father Baker as the vicar-general of the Buffalo diocese. Thus began a close association and friendship which ended only with Bishop Colton's death, and a high position in the administration of the diocese which Father Baker retained until his death in 1936.

He also served as administrator of the Buffalo diocese twice during vacancies in the see: from May 9, 1915, to June 17, 1916; and from July 9, 1918, to March 30, 1919.

Father Baker was made a domestic prelate, with the title of Right Reverend Monsignor, by Pope St. Pius X in 1905, and Prothonotary Apostolic by Pope Pius XI in 1922.

These ecclesiastical honors were important, of course, in reflecting the appreciation of the Church for Father Baker's tremendous works of charity through the assistance of Our Lady of Victory. The position of vicar-general added more burdens, but Father Baker always seemed to have plenty of time for everyone as he went his way, seemingly unperturbed and unruffled by added responsibilities.

As vicar-general, he was in effect second in command to the Bishop, and not unconscious of the additional influence this gave to him. He had the opportunity of advising the Bishop in the transfer of priests, in the naming of new pastors, and filling vacancies due to the death of pastors.

One story told about Father Baker may illustrate that he had a keen awareness of the possibilities of this situation. After his magnificent shrine to Our Lady of Victory had been completed, many of the young couples of Lackawanna — even from other parishes — wanted to be married there. Father Baker did not discourage this. He was more than willing to allow it. Some of the other pastors in Lackawanna, however, did not have the same attitude; they felt that marriages of their parishioners should be performed in the parish church.

One of them finally approached Father Baker and protested. "It isn't right, Monsignor. These people belong to my parish, and they should be married there."

Father Baker smiled softly, and pulled at his nose in a characteristic gesture. "We do not seek them out, Father. They come to us and ask permission to be married in the shrine to Our Lady of Victory. I do not have the heart to refuse them — they love the beauty of our basilica, as I do myself."

"You should send them away," the priest sputtered. "They should go to their own pastor, to their own parish church. Why don't you do that?"

Father Baker's smile remained, but he looked sharply at the other priest. Then he spoke, his voice as soft as ever. "What's the matter, Father? Don't you like it here in Lackawanna?" The subject was not raised again.

The issue of *The Victorian* for March, 1901, the year of Father Baker's silver jubilee in the priesthood, had a strangely prophetic tone. Writing of the new buildings and additions constructed by Father Baker, the editorial article noted: "It may be said now that the institutions at Victoria are complete . . . but it will be very strange if the next few years do not witness the erection of new buildings." *The Victorian* noted that Father Baker was then able to care for 1500 boys, who had come from almost every state in the Union. "Maine, North Carolina, Virginia, Colorado, Arkansas, Iowa are but a few of the states represented." There were even boys at Father Baker's who were natives of Ireland, England, France, and Canada.

"As a rule," the article continued, "these children come here alone, with a tag on a button and labeled, 'To Father Baker, Victoria, West Seneca, N. Y.' We have yet to hear of a little boy — some who came being only about six years old — getting lost. Not long since a six-year-old boy was placed upon a train in Philadelphia and arrived here on time; another came from Denver, Colorado; another from Norfolk, Virginia; another from Hot Springs, Arkansas."

How did all this come about? Father Baker's Association of Our Lady of Victory had spread all over the country. He had friends in every state — and, as *The Victorian* noted, "It is to their anxiety to save the Faith of these little boys that they are picked up and sent to the Home." Needless to say, Father Baker never turned them away.

One dark night, a distressed mother with two young boys came out to West Seneca, seeking help from Father Baker.

"I don't know what to do, Father," she said slowly. "My husband is dead. We just came here because he had been offered a good job. Now he is dead — and we have nothing."

"You have two fine boys," Father Baker told her quickly, "and what fine boys they are, too!" And then he began to talk to the boys, asking them questions about their schooling and the games they played. Soon the boys were much at ease, and after a bit a smile began to turn up the corners of the mother's tired mouth.

"Now then," said Father Baker to the mother, "we must do something about your problem."

"We have no place to live," the mother told him simply. "We have no money. I must find some work to do — but first, I must also find someone who will care for my children while I work."

Father Baker pulled a small statue from his pocket and handed it to her. "Our Lady of Victory will take care of you," he said, and then he gave each of the boys a medal of Our Lady of Victory. "She has done everything for us. We will find room for all of you tonight. And then tomorrow, I'm sure the Sisters of St. Joseph across the street will need another cook in the kitchen, or someone to help in the laundry — and that will be work for you. Caring for your two fine boys will be no problem. They can live at St. Joseph's, where the Sisters will care for them — and where you will be close to them."

The mother, close to tears, started to thank him, but Father Baker held up his hand and said, "No, no — this is all due to Our Lady of Victory." He called one of the Brothers, who happened to be going past the office, and asked him to find a room where the mother and her two boys could spend the night.

"Father," the Brother protested, "we haven't got an empty room. We've even got cots out in the halls where the boys are sleeping. There's not an inch of space that isn't being used."

"There must be," said Father Baker firmly, "there must be some room that could be used for this fine family."

The Brother shook his head. "We've had boys coming in from everywhere, it seems, and all the beds and cots have been put into use. In a day or two —"

"That isn't soon enough," Father Baker replied. He pulled at his nose for a moment or two in reflection, while the worried look returned to the mother's face. Then he cried, "Of course! Brother, please take this lady and her two boys down to the Sister who has charge of my room. Tell her to put them in my bedroom for the evening. Then in the morning we'll be able to make other arrangements."

"But, Father," protested the mother.

"But nothing," Father Baker answered with a smile. "Our Lady of Victory will provide. Now go along with Brother. I'm sure all of us can stand a good night's rest." And before she knew it, the mother and her two children were walking down the hall with the Brother.

"Brother," she said firmly, "we can't do this."

The Brother smiled and shook his head. "Can't is a word that Father Baker doesn't believe in. He would feel very hurt if you didn't — and besides, where will you go?"

"But where will he sleep?"

"Sometimes I wonder if he sleeps at all," said the Brother. "I've gone to bed when he was still working in his office, and in the morning found him kneeling in the chapel before Our Lady of Victory. Father Baker has reduced his personal needs to the bare minimum. You saw how slender he is. He eats very little. And it seems he needs — or allows himself — very little sleep."

"But, Brother," the woman persisted, "he must sleep. Where will he get his rest?"

The Brother hesitated, and then said, "You probably won't rest if you don't feel he'll be all right. Did you see that easy chair in his office? Often he will sit down there at night to say his Office, and drop asleep until morning. I imagine

80

that's what he'll do — unless he has some very difficult problems. When he does, he spends most of the night in the chapel, talking to Our Lady of Victory."

During the next few years, Father Baker added to the Protectory buildings and to the trade schools, built an infant home for abandoned and neglected babies, and then a large hospital and nurses home. But in all of this building, and his many duties as the head of it all, he never lost his interest in the boys.

Behind the Protectory building was a large yard, where the boys played. Whenever Father Baker stepped out into the yard, there was a big yell and all the boys would flock toward him. Then he would stroll around the yard and watch the games in progress.

Every once in a while, one of the bigger boys would hit a ball really hard — and crash! There would be a broken window. Some people were inclined to blame the boys for that, and would complain to Father Baker. He would look at them, flash his famous smile, and say, "Well, we've got some glass somewhere around. Where there are boys and windows, you have two items of expense you can't get away from — bread and glass!"

On Sundays he would take a group of the boys on a long walk along the country roads. Sometimes a farmer would come along and offer a ride. Then Father Baker would call out, "Come on — let's keep this gentleman company for a while!" And all would climb up on the hayrack and have a bumpy ride down the road for a mile or two. In the fall, when the apples were ripe, Father Baker would stop at a farmhouse and buy a bushel of apples, and the boys would have their caps, pockets, and shirts full of apples to eat on the way.

Every week the boys saw the best of the movies that were available, with Father Baker often enjoying the pictures with them. Many of the famous movie stars of those days used to come out to Our Lady of Victory Homes to see Father Baker and to give the boys a special treat.

81

It often seemed as though Father Baker was always trying to think up outings for the boys. He would take them on trips to Niagara Falls, for a ride on a lake steamer; and for years he would have the boys taken to the lake for swimming, about fifty at a time. But then he decided it would be better to have a swimming pool right at the Homes. He got a contractor to build it, and the boys had swimming without having to travel to the lake for it. One of the highlights of the year was the annual auto ride and picnic. Members of the Automobile Club of Buffalo would come to Our Lady of Victory Homes, load the boys into their cars, and take them to a city park. There they would get all the hot dogs, ice cream, and soda they wanted.

Even in the very early days, when there was not much to do things with at the Homes, Father Baker saw that all the boys were remembered at Christmas time. All the desks would be taken out of one of the classrooms, and a big Christmas tree put up. The Sisters of St. Joseph would pass around candy, popcorn, and peanuts to the boys, and then Father Baker would call out their names. As each one came forward, Father Baker would give him the present with his name on it. Often these were not large presents, because there were so many places for the money to go, but each boy was remembered, individually and specially.

For the summer months, Father Baker established camp for the boys, some miles away, where they lived in tents and enjoyed an outdoor life. The boys would go down for a week or two at a time, and enjoy the great outdoors, playing cowboy and Indian, or tracking rabbits and other game through the woods — or just enjoying themselves away from the regular routine of life. Father Baker also maintained a farm, just behind the Homes, where cows and chickens, geese and ducks provided food for the boys. Here too were gardens where vegetables were grown for the tables at Our Lady of Victory Homes.

There was a heavy load of incoming mail at Our Lady of

Victory Homes, and this brought its share of problems, too. It soon became common knowledge throughout the area that much money was coming to Father Baker through the mails. Stories began to circulate about hundred dollar bills coming to him in plain envelopes, and smaller bills, of course. In fact, the bulk of Father Baker's support came through the mail. In most instances, this came in the form of money orders and checks, but even these sometimes were not completely safe. Once a post-office clerk obtained some money orders sent to Father Baker and cashed them himself. When this was discovered, he was immediately discharged. However, Father Baker learned of it, and took what he considered the most appropriate action, somewhat to the surprise of those who did not know him well. He offered the young man a job in one of his departments at the institutions. This was characteristic of Father Baker. He was a keen-minded and alert businessman, but all of his actions were bedded deep in a Christlike charity.

He had an amazing memory for details, as more than one salesman discovered. One had called to sell food supplies and was showing samples of some beans. Father Baker took a handful and ran them through his fingers as he studied them.

"How much are these?" he asked.

"Six cents a pound."

"They were five and a half last year, but I know the price has gone up. That's fair. We'll take — " and he ordered the amount required.

As Brother Stanislaus would say, "Father Baker was a one-man show. He did everything himself. He would do all the buying." And then Brother Stanislaus would add, "except for the printing business, after he found out that I knew how to run it."

CHAPTER XI

THE year 1903 seems to be the first year in which the Litany of Our Blessed Lady of Victory was published in the *Annals*. It was composed for private devotion by Brother Francis, the third Brother to join the Brothers of the Holy Infancy, who had come to Limestone Hill about 1867. He had been a Dominican novice in Ireland before coming to the United States.

Published with the Litany was a prayer which Father Baker himself had composed, and which he recited after each low Mass. It read: "O Victorious Lady! thou who hast ever such powerful influence with thy Divine Son in conquering the hardest of hearts, intercede for those for whom we pray, that their hearts being softened by the rays of Divine Grace, they may return to the unity of the true Faith, through Christ Our Lord. Amen."

The institutions had been prospering; true, the income was never too great at any one time, but the clients of Our Lady of Victory kept it coming through the mail. Perhaps now was the time to build the church Father Baker had wanted for a long time, to replace old St. Patrick's Church as well as give further honor to Our Lady of Victory. Still, he hesitated, because he felt that there might be a greater need.

Frequently, stories had appeared in the newspapers about the bodies of infants being found in different parts of the city, apparently abandoned by their mothers, who often were unmarried. The babies had been left to die, because their mothers could find no place, no one to care for them. One day Father Baker picked up the day's newspaper and re-read the story that had brought back this subject so vividly. In cleaning out an old canal, dredges had dug up the bones and bodies of infants and small children drowned in the waters of the canal through the years. Something must be done to save the souls, and the lives themselves, of these innocent little children.

Father Baker remembered a widow, Mrs. Amelia Mathieson, whom he had met just a few days before. She had a rooming house down in Buffalo. She was a kindhearted and sensible soul, Father Baker knew, and she had a few spare rooms.

Not long after, Father Baker was talking to her. "You have some spare rooms, I think you told me."

"Oh, yes, Father."

"I'd like to rent them."

"Rent them? Father Baker, you're joking!"

"Oh, no," he said seriously. "I am very concerned about these babies and small children who are being abandoned almost daily, left in empty lots to die, or thrown into the canal to drown. If you could rent me your empty rooms, and if you would help care for them, we could open a home for infants, and have the opportunity of saving their souls and their lives. Will you help me?"

"Of course, Father," she replied, and so the home for infants was begun.

As word passed around that Father Baker had opened such a home, it did not take long to fill the vacant rooms. At first the babies were put on the large beds of the former roomers; then cribs replaced these beds. Mrs. Mathieson, in later days, would tell how Father Baker came there to help set up the cribs. Soon the flow of infants so increased that the regular roomers were moved out, and Father Baker could see that even larger quarters would be necessary.

85

Thus, in 1906, he announced plans to build an infants' home at Victorhill. It would cost more than $100,000, be of brick construction, with a frontage of 150 feet along Ridge Road across from the Protectory. The building would have two wings running back 144 feet on each side, with a court between.

Writing in the *Annals* of July, 1906, Father Baker said that he hoped "to have it under roof before the winter, and the following summer will see it dedicated to Almighty God under the kind protection of Our Dear Lady of Victory. Our work will then be complete. This Infant Home will be for children from infancy to five years of age; our Orphan Home from five to ten, and our Protectory from ten to fifteen; then our Working Boys' Home will care for those over fifteen years of age, so that every class will be well protected, from infancy to maturity."

A news story in the West Seneca *Bulletin* about the same time reported that when the infants' home was completed and paid for, "the subject of a new church for St. Patrick's parish may come up again for consideration, it having now been put aside. It is known by Father Baker's best friends that he is ambitious of giving his parish here one of the greatest churches in the world before his earthly cares are ended and he is called to his reward for his saintly works."

The cornerstone of the new building was laid on March 25, 1907, and Father Baker, in the *Annals*, kept his friends and supporters advised as to its progress. He was keenly aware of the value of pictures, and frequently used architects' drawings and photographs of the work in progress.

That same year Father Baker adopted a suggestion, which has had a strong appeal throughout the years to those wanting to help the infants at Our Lady of Victory Homes. It was the offer to furnish a crib in the infants' home. In the *Annals* for April, 1907, Father Baker wrote:

"Some of our friends expressed a wish to furnish a little crib for one of the infants, and we are pleased at the sug-

86

gestion, and will give all those an opportunity who desire to furnish a little crib, mattress, pillows and bedding, by contributing the sum of $25.00, when they will be remembered also in all the Masses offered in the Home, as well as the pious prayers of the Sisters and children, besides having their names engraven upon a brass tablet placed upon the wall, which will keep them in constant remembrances, and Almighty God will not fail to abundantly bless them, for He has promised that 'Whatsoever you do to the least of these, My little ones, you do it to Me.' "

Again in the *Annals* for October, 1907, Father Baker said that so many infants had been sent to the home that he could hardly care for them because of the limited accommodations. "Our pleasure will be great, when we can notify our good friends that our building is completed and we are ready to receive all little ones that may be presented."

To this he added: "It is astonishing, the number of applications we have had to receive them, and these come from the poor abandoned and destitute mother, the penniless widow, or the unfortunate creature, with no place to lay her fatherless child; there is no question of the vast amount of good that must necessarily come from such a work, and there is no doubt that God wishes it. . . ."

The building was finished and dedicated on August 16, 1908. It was to become one of the greater interests of Father Baker, for he went there almost every evening to play with the infants and to bless them. It also inspired the formation of the Our Lady of Victory Aid Society, organized in October, 1908, with its object of "making and providing articles of clothing for the infants and small children of Our Lady of Victory Infant Home." The ladies of this society were untiring in their work.

The Sisters of St. Joseph provided the Sister personnel for the infants' home, and in this — as in all of Father Baker's works — they proved to be mighty collaborators with him in the cause of Our Lady of Victory.

One of the fixtures at the infants' home was a small bassinet, complete with pillows and blankets, that stood in the hallway, just inside the door. Any distressed mother could quietly open the door in the middle of the night and leave her baby in the bassinet, with no questions asked, no forms to fill out, no probing into her or the baby's background. For a number of years, the bassinet stayed there, and any abandoned baby soon made its presence known. One of the Sisters of St. Joseph always came quickly to take care of it.

Father Baker's routine was almost set by now. Each day, after his administrative work was done, he would go over to the infants' home and visit with the babies. He would go from ward to ward, holding the bottle for one baby, covering another's feet, patting the cheek of another. Then, when he had concluded his rounds, he would stand in the doorway and bless the babies and the nurses for the night.

Before going over to the hospital which was later built next to the infants' home, he would stand at a window overlooking Holy Cross Cemetery and pray for the souls of those buried there. Then he would go to the hospital and visit with the patients.

At the infants' home occurred some of those amazing and unexplainable happenings in what has been called Father Baker's "miracle-filled life." The phrase comes from a letter which the then Bishop Thomas Joseph Walsh of Newark, later Archbishop of Newark, sent to his priests announcing the death of Father Baker and asking their prayers for the repose of his soul.

One of the unusual happenings at the infants' home concerned Mrs. Josephine Pilkington, then 18 years old, and secretary to Brother Stanislaus at The Victorian magazine. She had been living in the Infant Home.

At the office on a hot September day, she began to get chills. Brother Stanislaus told her to go to the Infant Home, but she insisted on finishing out the day. That night her appendix ruptured. As they carried her on a stretcher from

88

her third-floor room at the Infant Home, on the way to the hospital, Father Baker unexpectedly happened along.

"Who is that?" he asked.

Sister St. Edward, the superior, replied, "That is Josephine, Father. Brother Stan's secretary."

"We must follow her," Father Baker said, and he went with the group to the hospital. There he heard Josephine's confession and then asked her if she were afraid to die.

The sick girl looked up and said, "No, Father, today or tomorrow — it doesn't make any difference. I am ready."

He put his hand on hers and said, "You are not going to die, Josephine. Don't be afraid. You have a mission in life and a lot of hard work ahead of you." As she tells the story today, Mrs. Pilkington adds a bit ruefully, "And he was so right."

As the crisis in the sickness approached, Josephine began to slip and the Sisters got quite concerned over her condition. One of them sent a nurse over to Father Baker with the message that if he wanted to see Josephine before she died and give her final absolution, he should come right away.

Father Baker was having his usual very light lunch. He looked up from his glass of milk and said, "Tell Sister not to get excited. Josephine isn't going to die."

And she didn't. That afternoon she took a turn for the better and soon recovered completely. Mrs. Pilkington adds, "And everybody, even the doctors, said I couldn't make it."

Another certainly unusual incident happened with a nurse in the Infant Home who came from New York City. She had become critically ill and her father was sent for because it was feared that she would not live.

The next day she was much worse. That evening, as the doctor examined her, he silently covered her face. The nurses began to cry and wail, as the doctor left the room.

Then in walked Father Baker. "What's the matter here?" he asked, in his usual soft tone.

One of the Sisters said, "Miss Clark is dead."

"We must say the Rosary for her," Father Baker said, and all the nurses and Sisters knelt around the bed. Father Baker uncovered her face, took her hand and as he prayed, kept his fingers on her pulse. One of the nurses next to him, a non-Catholic, said later that she thought he was "crazy."

When the Rosary was finished, Father Baker turned to the non-Catholic nurse and said, "Take her pulse."

"But, Father," the girl protested, "she is dead."

"Take her pulse anyway," Father Baker insisted.

The nurse did as she was told — and the sick girl was alive. In the excitement of all this, Father Baker quietly left the room. The sick girl recovered completely from her critical illness.

Shortly after the Infant Home was completed, the Lackawanna Steel Company moved to West Seneca. About that time, a dispute arose between the eastern and western sections of the town over payment for certain improvements, and as a result the area around Limestone Hill formed its own city. As names for this new municipality were considered, Father Baker again suggested Victory, but the final choice was Lackawanna, and so it was incorporated in 1909.

In the years to come, the operation of Our Lady of Victory Infant Home was to bring Father Baker into sharp conflict with the authorities of New York State who had the responsibility for inspecting charitable institutions. It was, in a rather unfortunate sense, a conflict between two different theories or principles of charity.

Father Baker felt the individual's need came first. His charitable institutions were open to anyone at any time and from any place. One priest told of calling Father Baker about a young woman from his city who was expecting a baby. Father Baker said, "Send her to us. We'll be happy to care for her." There was no question about who would pay for her care. Father Baker's first thought went to the individual, and he knew that Our Lady of Victory would provide the needed funds. This priest added, "If I should have any money when I die, I want it to go to Father Baker for his charities."

Father Baker's first consideration in the case of an unwed mother was to safeguard the reputation of the mother and her family. Some of the authorities wanted him to reveal the names and home addresses of these unmarried mothers, but Father Baker steadfastly refused to do so.

There were also disputes over adoption procedures, some of the authorities feeling that Father Baker did not have a thorough enough investigation made of prospective adoptive parents, and also that there was not a careful "follow-up" procedure, after the child had been placed in such a home.

Undoubtedly there was merit on both sides of the question. Much of this criticism, expressed mostly in reports to various state departments, was concerned with compliance with various regulations. Some of these were important; others seemed to be relatively minor matters.

Father Baker's replies to these reports — if he did reply — have been lost through the years, and all that remain are copies of the investigators' remarks. But time after time, the reports would note that changes had been made "as suggested in previous report."

In Father Baker's later years, there seems no question but that he was not able to supervise all these charitable activities as closely as he had done in younger years, and perhaps there may have been some deterioration in the quality of the care being given. This came partly from the fact that Father Baker had never learned to delegate authority in major matters. For so many years it had been, as Brother Stanislaus said, "a one-man show," and that one man was no longer able to run the whole show. Few men live into the nineties, and few of these retain their vigor and effectiveness until their last days. Father Baker kept his vigor and his effective managing ability longer than most men in their middle nineties, but the drop, when it did come, came suddenly in the last year or two of his life.

CHAPTER XII

FATHER BAKER'S next big project was Our Lady of Victory Hospital. In the *Annals* for January, 1911, he wrote that during the previous two years, "over 700 little helpless babes have been given shelter and protection, and many have been adopted into good Catholic homes." Then he added: "We never realized before entering into this work the great demand that would be made upon us to care for this class of homeless little ones."

While he never said it, either in writing or in talking with others, he was subjected to some bitter criticism over the Infant Home. There were those who felt that he was condoning sin or making things "too easy" for the unfortunate unwed mothers. These criticisms were never voiced to Father Baker, of course; but even if they had been, they would not have deterred his actions. Father Baker, for all of his mildness, his kindly manner and soft-spoken conversation, had an iron determination when he knew something needed doing for Our Lady of Victory — and for God's children.

In 1914, Father Baker announced that it was necessary to make a large addition to the Infant Home. "The reason for this new work," he wrote in the *Annals*, "is that our Infant Home is filled to its utmost capacity, and unless we add more room, we must stop taking babies and small children, and this we do not wish to do."

The cornerstone for the new building, to be an infant home

and maternity hospital, was laid on August 15, 1915. However, the building was not opened until October 2, 1919. A disastrous fire in January, 1916, destroyed the boys' orphan home, which then had to be rebuilt. The expenses of the Our Lady of Victory institutions had grown year by year, too. During the previous year the expenses had been more than $125,000. The income from public and private sources for the institutions was only about half that amount, leaving a deficit, Father Baker reported, of $62,396.53. This was eventually made up from the charitable donations which he received through the Association of Our Lady of Victory and from other sources.

The new infant home and maternity hospital was to cost nearly $250,000, and now the orphan home had to be rebuilt. As always, Father Baker in times like these had recourse to Our Lady of Victory and to her friends; and, as always, they did not fail him.

It may have been during a time of financial stress like this that Brother Stanislaus observed Father Baker walking down the hall with a piece of paper in his hand. Brother Stanislaus was off to the side, where he could not be readily seen, so he watched Father Baker stop at the statue of Our Lady of Victory in the hall, glance quickly around to see if anyone was within sight, and then slip the white piece of paper under the statue.

Then he looked up at the statue of Our Lady of Victory, as if talking to it, patted the little Infant in her arms, and walked away. Brother Stanislaus, a few days later, asked Father Baker about the incident. "You know, Father," he said hesitantly, "I saw you in the hall the other day, putting a piece of paper under the statue of Our Lady of Victory."

"Oh?" Father Baker's eyes lit up, and he waited expectantly.

"Why did you do that?"

Father Baker smiled, tipped his head to the right, and looked up at the ceiling. Brother Stanislaus waited patiently.

"Oh, that!" said Father Baker, still smiling. "That was a

bill we couldn't meet ourselves, and so I asked her to take care of it."

"And did she?"

Father Baker reached out and affectionately patted Brother Stanislaus on the cheek, as he often did to people he liked. "Of course, Brother. You know she did."

The maternity hospital, from its beginning, had included a nursing school, but the hospital itself was intended only for the unwed mothers, who could thus have the privacy and special care they needed. State legislation in 1920 required, however, that registered nurses obtain their training in a hospital whose patients included men, women, and children, and in which surgical and disease cases received treatment.

But even before this, Father Baker had been urged to turn the hospital into a general one. Dr. Michael Sullivan, one of "Father Baker's boys," led the doctors in urging the necessity of such a hospital in the Our Lady of Victory institutions, and so did the Sisters of St. Joseph. Dr. Sullivan had even organized a group of doctors who met every two or three weeks to discuss and exchange medical ideas. Father Baker found he had a medical staff for his new hospital right at hand.

In Our Lady of Victory Hospital, hundreds of residents of Lackawanna and Buffalo receive excellent care each year. There, too, the name of Father Baker and his manifold charities is perpetuated. Sometimes this is vividly brought home to administrators at the hospital; even today, for instance, as in the case of an Indian who had been injured while working on his small farm. His family brought him to Our Lady of Victory Hospital, even though he lived quite a distance away. They said quite frankly, "We have no money, no hospitalization. But people say when you cannot pay, go to Father Baker's hospital!"

That same year of 1919, when the hospital opened, saw a bitter steel strike that vitally affected many of the people in Lackawanna, and of course many of them were Father

94

Baker's parishioners. Conditions in the steel industry at that time were much different from what they are today. One report declared that the average work week for all employees was 68.7 hours; that the corporations' "arbitrary control of hours and wages" extended to everything in individual jobs, causing daily grievances; that the company control extended even outside the plant, affecting "workers as citizens and the social institutions in the communities"; and that "efforts were made to influence the local press, pulpit and police authorities."

Those days, happily, are now long gone, but the conditions did exist in those bitter days of 1919, and feelings ran very high on both sides of the controversy. The men, many of whom lived in "company houses" owned by the steel corporation, went on strike. They were told, very plainly and very bluntly, to go back to work or get out of the company houses. The men did not go back to work and as a result they were locked out of their homes, many of them with large families.

Father Baker, as the leading figure in the community, knew what was going on and sent for the men. He found houses for many of them in other parts of Lackawanna, paid the rent, furnished food for them, and helped them exist during the crisis of the strike. As the men came to see him, he would give them four, five, or six loaves of bread — whatever they needed — and to each a silver dollar.

As had happened before, and as was to happen time and time again, some people protested to Father Baker. One said, "Father Baker, you shouldn't do that. These men — or some of them — are taking you for a ride."

Father Baker smiled, and told the man softly, "Any man who takes the money and the bread needs it, or he wouldn't be here." And that was that. One man who was in the 1919 steel strike declared, "If you got in line a dozen times, Father Baker would give you that silver dollar."

Pressure from the local municipal authorities was used in an effort to stop Father Baker from helping the men. This too was ineffective, for he told them very plainly, "I am doing this." Father Baker's influence in the community was not to be underestimated, and it was "hands off" from then on.

Some of the men in the steel strike had to leave town to find work in order to support their families. They worked in Detroit, Chicago, or Gary, Indiana, and very often they would get to talking about their home town. Always the question would come: "Do you know Father Baker?" And if you said "Yes," and told them that you had been raised by Father Baker, you could get anything you wanted.

Many of the boys at Father Baker's went on to fame and fortune. Some of his "graduates" served in Congress and as governors of various states; some became vice-presidents of large corporations; and a large number became priests, inspired no doubt by Father Baker himself.

Even today, the Sisters of St. Joseph will tell you, a priest may drop in at the Basilica or at the Orphans' Home, and tell them that he lived there as a boy. Doctors and lawyers and judges, too, can trace their lives back to the happy days they spent at Father Baker's Homes, where they got their education and training. Father Baker had added a high school to his buildings; and for those boys who had the ability and the desire, he was always willing to help them go on to college or to the seminary.

This was all done so quietly that few persons knew about it, except the boys themselves. Father Baker himself was quite embarrassed at a reception given him in his later years, when a prominent Buffalo attorney got up and publicly thanked him for sending him through college and law school. "You didn't have to say that," Father Baker told him. "You didn't have to say it."

Besides the more prominent graduates of Father Baker's, there are thousands more who are living fine lives, whose splendid families show how well they absorbed the training they got from Father Baker, from the Brothers of the Holy Infancy, and from the Sisters of St. Joseph. As one of the

Brothers says, "Are not these men successful too? They have good jobs, own their own homes, and have fine families — what more could you ask?"

Often these families come back to Lackawanna, so that the father can show his family where he was raised. And often the mother of the family will take one of the Sisters of St. Joseph aside and say, "My husband always talks about Father Baker's. It is the only childhood home he remembers, and I'm so grateful for what you've done for him."

There are many tributes to Father Baker, some of them erected in stone, in magnificent buildings; but perhaps even more enduring are those which he erected in the hearts of thousands of boys who might never have had a chance at decent lives without him.

The year 1921 saw the beginning of Father Baker's dream project, the building of the national shrine to Our Lady of Victory. He had hoped to build it before, but then the Orphans' Home was destroyed by fire and he had to put that dream away. Now he felt ready to begin.

He called a meeting of the men of the parish to tell them about it. One of the men still recalls how Father Baker announced the plans: "Father Baker explained that he was starting a shrine to Our Lady of Victory, and there wouldn't be anything in the world — let alone the country — that could compare with it."

Then Father Baker said, "We haven't got a nickel to start, and we won't have a nickel left to pay on it when it is finished."

Father Baker made his first appeal for help in building the shrine in the *Annals*, the publication of the Association of Our Lady of Victory, and thousands of our Lady's friends rallied to the project. He secured the best architect, the best artist, and the best builder he could for this, and soon the work began. This was to be his great building effort, a magnificent tribute to Our Lady of Victory from him and from all those who had been aided by her through the past years.

Father Baker was then nearly eighty years old, yet his energy and his determination far exceeded those of many younger men. Few men at his age would have dared start such a project, but Father Baker knew that Our Lady of Victory would help him, and he had no fears.

The beautiful shrine was erected on the site of the old St. Patrick's Church, alongside the Protectory building, and across from the boys' orphan home. A magnificent Renaissance structure, it has two large towers and a great dome. Over the main entrance is a 16,000-pound statue of Our Lady of Victory in marble.

Two columns of pillars go out in a semicircle from the main entrance, and atop the end of each is a group of figures — one a number of children gathered around a Sister, and the other another group around a priest.

Father Baker's plan was that the figure of the Sister would symbolize the work of the Sisters of St. Joseph with the children at Our Lady of Victory Homes. The figure of the priest would symbolize the work of the priests and the Brothers of the Holy Infancy there. Neither one was to represent a particular Sister or a particular priest.

However, as you stand on Ridge Road in Lackawanna and look up at the figure of the priest, you know that it represents Father Baker. The statues were carved in Italy, and when they arrived in Lackawanna for installation, Father Baker was horrified to find that he had been carved in stone. He protested, but was told there was no way to change it now — the figures would have to go up as they were, or the place would have to stand vacant. Reluctantly, Father Baker agreed to let the statuary be put in place.

Some of his co-workers at Our Lady of Victory Homes had conspired against Father Baker. They had worked with the artist secretly, because they knew that he would never permit his representation in the group if he did know about it. But they also felt that he should be represented in this beautiful shrine, and that Our Lady of Victory would want it so. While

98

Father Baker inspected the work on the shrine day after day, a young Italian artist would be off to the side, modeling his face in clay. When the work was finished, the model was sent to Italy, where the marble carvers fashioned the statue — and there was Father Baker!

Thousands of people all over the country sent their contributions to help build this national shrine to Our Lady of Victory. Most of these were small ones — $10 for blocks of the white marble used to build it — though there were many very substantial donations.

One man in Lackawanna recalls Father Baker himself going from door to door securing contributions for the monstrance, the gold-plated receptacle used for Benediction and for exposition of the Blessed Sacrament. Father Baker came to his house seeking gold and silver, diamonds and jewelry of any kind, that could be melted down. "My grandmother's wedding ring and my mother's wedding and engagement rings are in the monstrance in the Basilica," he says proudly.

CHAPTER **XIII**

THE national shrine to Our Lady of Victory had its first services at Christmas time in 1925, with the annual novena beginning on December 17 and ending on Christmas day. Writing about this opening event in the *Annals*, Father Baker described the beautiful shrine and said: "The spirit of Our Lady permeates the entire edifice" — as, indeed, it does.

The magnificent dome before the main altar features four beautifully twisted columns of red Pyrenese marble. A striking story lies behind them, according to Francis H. Van Eich, manager of the religious-goods studio at the shrine, who is one of "Father Baker's boys," and proud of it, as all of them are. Van Eich told the story to Josephine Pilkington, who recorded it in *The Victorian* for May, 1945.

After World War I, some soldiers made a side trip into Spain, just to see what the country was like. In the group were some Buffalo soldiers, who were quite astonished to find in a country cottage a picture of Our Lady of Victory and one of Father Baker. The Buffalo men tried to make the farmer understand that they were from Buffalo, and that they knew Father Baker.

However, he could not understand English and went to get a neighbor who did. Through the translator, they explained that they lived near the homes which Father Baker had established, and that they knew him well. Then one mentioned that some time Father Baker wanted to build a beautiful church for Our Lady of Victory, with the marble to be imported from Italy, France, and Greece.

The elderly farmer became quite excited. Through the interpreter, he told the soldiers that he had some rare red marble on his own property. He had been unable to find anyone interested enough to quarry it, but if Father Baker wanted it for his beautiful church honoring Our Lady of Victory, he could have it for nothing!

When the soldiers finally got back to Buffalo, they told the story to Father Baker. When he was ready to proceed with the national shrine for Our Lady of Victory and his architect was abroad contracting for the materials, Father Baker asked him to visit the Spanish farmer. The architect carefully inspected the outcropping of marble, and was convinced that excavation of it would be worthwhile. This was done, and the rock formation proved just large enough to obtain the four pieces that now serve to beautify the main altar in the shrine to Our Lady of Victory.

The shrine was completed by the contractor, Edward S. Jordan, another of Father Baker's good friends; and the date was set for its dedication — May 25, 1926, the same year in which Father Baker celebrated the golden jubilee of his ordination.

Then, on July 20, 1926, to quote the words of *L'Osservatore Romano*, the Vatican City daily newspaper, "a very distinguished and rare privilege" was given it. By Apostolic Decree, Pope Benedict XV elevated the shrine to the dignity of a basilica, one of the few in the United States. The decree stated:

> Among the churches of America, the Sanctuary of Our Lady of Victory is for many reasons to be counted as one of the greatest. It is solemnly consecrated to God in the city of Lackawanna, in the confines of the diocese of Buffalo. This sanctuary had its origin in an old church wherein was a statue of the Blessed Virgin with the Infant Jesus in her arms, famed for miracles, and held in veneration near and far. Indeed such

101

crowds gathered to it from the whole United States, that the shrine became all too small to contain them. Hence the former building was demolished and a new one erected on the same site through the zealous efforts of Our Beloved Son, Nelson H. Baker, Prothonotary Apostolic and Vicar General of the Diocese of Buffalo. After nearly fifty years of unflagging labor, he finished the great enterprise, a splendid monument of piety and of civic munificence. This sanctuary is truly a masterpiece, in the nobility of its lines, in the splendor of its marbles, in its massive solidarity and in its artistic finish. . . .

This sanctuary is celebrated for its pilgrimages, necessitating the services of a number of priests. It is rich in its furnishings, and the devotions are carried out with great magnificence. The Popes have granted it many indulgences and privileges, and its confraternities are numerous. Above all, there is one — that of Our Lady of Victory — numbering over 100,000 members, worthy of special mention as a national institution, abounding in works of Christian charity. It is also worthy of note, that though great sums of money have been expended in building and adorning the sacred edifice, and in supporting the works connected with it, there is at present no debt on the whole, a remarkable sign of unstinting charity, and a testimony to the fatherly Providence of God in its regard.

Taking all this into consideration, at the prayer of Our Venerable Brother, Thomas Joseph Walsh, the Bishop of Trenton, Assistant at the Pontifical Throne, at present in the Holy City and voicing in the Roman Curia the wishes of Our Venerable Brother, William Turner, the Bishop of Buffalo, and of the clergy and people of both dioceses, and of all America, insistently praying that we deign to raise this sanctuary to the dignity of a Minor Basilica, we have thought it well to accede freely and of our own accord to these instances.

Having consulted therefore with Our Venerable Brother, Anthony Cardinal Vico, Bishop of Porto and Santa Rufina, the prefect of the Sacred Congregation of Rites, unto the glory and honor of the illustrious sanctuary, to manifest our loving interest in its supporters, and munificent benefactors, as also to console and rejoice the body of the faithful who give such singular proof of their devotion to the Virgin Mother of God, Our Lady of Victory, and her holy image with the Infant Jesus, of our own accord, with certain knowledge and after mature deliberation, in the fulness of our apostolic authority, in virtue of the present letters and in perpetuity, we bestow upon the church or sanctuary of the Blessed Virgin Our Lady of Victory, situated in the city of Lackawanna, in the diocese of Buffalo, the title and dignity of a Minor Basilica, with all the honors and privileges rightfully and of custom to Minor Basilicas appertaining. . . .

The article in *L'Osservatore Romano* on July 28, 1926, called the shrine of Our Lady of Victory "one of the most superb shrines that the Catholic Church possesses in the United States. . . .

"But it is not its beauty, size and magnificence that gives to the Sanctuary of Our Lady of Victory of Lackawanna its greatest importance. Its greatest value is that it is the center of a very large work of piety and charity and from it radiates a network of splendid benefactions that extend to all the States of the Union and binds together in spiritual ties thousands and thousands of fervent Catholics who in their devotions to the Virgin there venerated find a powerful food of their faith.

"In fact, around the Sanctuary are grouped a number of vast edifices devoted to the most varied and useful works of charity, such as hospitals, orphanages, houses of maternity, asylums, workshops, schools, foundling homes, in a word, a little world of charity in which only in the last year have been received at least 2,850 beneficiaries, babies, children, patients, unmarried mothers. It is in fact truly 'a national work of charity,' and as such was recognized by President Coolidge, during its construction, on the occasion of the request of exemption of duty for the marble that was to be used in its erection."

Memories of Father Baker permeate every corner of the beautiful Basilica to Our Lady of Victory. In its basement, a replica of his living quarters has been arranged.

Every day visitors come to see this section of the Basilica, which might almost be called a little shrine to Father Baker. Here have been assembled the personal effects and furniture of the great man who aided so many thousands throughout his long and fruitful life, through the help of Our Lady of Victory.

In the bedroom of the replica is the huge old-fashioned brass bed, with Father Baker's picture of Our Lady of Victory hanging on the wall over it. Included also are the Mother of Sorrows altar and kneeling bench, gas fireplace, the old-fashioned radio which he occasionally used, and a six-foot wall crucifix, a gift to Father Baker from the Carmelite Sisters in Buffalo.

Many of the stories told about Father Baker center about the Basilica of Our Lady of Victory. He would spend much time there, especially in the evenings, kneeling before the Sacred Heart altar, where perpetual adoration of the Blessed Sacrament was maintained.

Father Baker was then in his late eighties, and it was a familiar sight to see him there. During the colder days, he often wore a heavy shawl around his shoulders, fastened with a huge safety pin. His vest pockets would hold a quantity of folded bills — one dollar, five dollars, ten dollars. As he knelt there, or as he entered or left the Basilica, often he would be approached by someone in need. Father Baker would listen quietly and then, glancing around to see that no one was watching, would inconspicuously hand the needy one a folded bill in whatever amount might be required, with a soft "God bless you."

As usual, there were some who criticized Father Baker's generosity, but he had a ready answer, which he liked to illustrate with a story. This happened during the depression days when the criticisms increased, especially when Father Baker helped everyone who came to him in need. He was never parochial in his charity. Everyone was God's creation, and Father Baker tried to help everyone in need.

"I've often been criticized," Father Baker told Henry W. Hilliard, an old friend, "for taking care of these poor people. But let's put ourselves in their position. Some of them may have been careless. Some may have been lazy and didn't want to work, and some maybe couldn't find work. They're hungry and cold. What would we do if we were hungry and cold and had no means to take care of ourselves? We would probably go to the corner store and steal a loaf of bread and a bottle of milk and get into trouble. We do this for these men to keep them from getting into trouble. And God is blessing our work. Times are hard, but we manage."

"I have also been criticized for giving out money to anyone who asks for it," said Father Baker. "Well, I find that the more we give away, the more we get. I'll give you an example. This morning I was on the corner and a poor lady stopped and said she was being put out of her home because she couldn't pay her rent. Well, you see this vest pocket? In it I always keep money for just such purposes. So I asked the lady how much she needed. She said she needed twelve dollars. I had just twelve dollars, so I gave it to her, and told her to pay the rent and enjoy her home for another month. She was very happy. It was the first time that that vest pocket was emptied. Then, just as I was entering the building, a man stepped up and pressed something into my hand and said, 'Here, Father, is something to do some good with,' and he was gone. I looked, and it was a twenty dollar bill. So you see, I gave away twelve dollars and received twenty. That's the way God works."

In the magnificent shrine, Father Baker often would kneel inside the sanctuary, spread his medals out before him on the kneeling bench, and then look up at the statue of Our Lady of Victory. Those who saw him there would feel that he was talking to Our Lady of Victory, and that he was hearing her talk to him. He would bless the medals and touch them and look up at the statue. Occasionally he would smile. Then he would put the medals in his pocket, and give them out to everyone who asked.

Many unusual and unexplainable cures were reported in the Basilica. One concerns a girl from Lockport, New York, who had been born a cripple. Her mother would bring her to Father Baker's for frequent visits, wheeling her through the shrine to Our Lady of Victory.

One summer afternoon, she brought the girl to the shrine as usual, and wheeled her to the Sacred Heart altar. Father Baker was kneeling there, and recognized the girl and her mother and came over to see them. "Do you still believe that our Lady will help you?" he asked the girl.

"I'm sure of it," she told him.

Then Father Baker took off the medal of Our Lady of Victory which he always wore pinned to the lapel of his coat, and pinned it to the girl's jacket. He said to the mother, "Wheel her around the shrine, behind the main altar, and show her all the other altars there. And then come back here."

The mother did as Father Baker requested. When she had finished the tour of the shrine, she came back to the Sacred Heart altar, where Father Baker was kneeling. The mother turned the wheel chair so that the girl was facing the altar — and the daughter suddenly screamed, stood up, and walked.

There were other people in the shrine, and they came rushing over to see what had happened. "I can walk! I can walk!" the girl cried, tears of joy streaming down her face. The mother, hardly able to talk with excitement, told the other people what had happened, and then turned to thank Father Baker. But he wasn't there. He had quietly slipped away in the excitement, silently thanking Our Lady of Victory for the cure.

CHAPTER XIV

AGE seemed not to diminish Father Baker's enthusiasm and desire to help those who were in need. No one could have found fault with the venerable priest if finally he decided that he had done enough. He had cared for thousands of infants, boys of all ages, unwed mothers, and the sick and needy of Lackawanna, of the surrounding area — and indeed, even from all parts of the United States — for Father Baker's charity was never bounded by geographic limits.

His eyes seemed as bright and as sharp as ever behind his rimless spectacles. Those who did not know him well hardly suspected that behind those spectacles was one glass eye, his own having been removed late in December, 1927. It was hard for many of his friends and assistants to understand why he had to undergo this affliction; yet Father Baker himself never complained.

One morning in December that year, Brother Thomas was driving him to Mt. St. Joseph in Buffalo, where, even in his eighty-fifth year, he was to say a Requiem Mass for his long-time friend, Mother Mary Anne Burke of the Sisters of St. Joseph. Father Baker's connections with the Sisters of St. Joseph were close and particularly friendly; their aid and generous co-operation had made much of his work possible, and Mother Mary Anne had been a very close friend.

As was his custom when riding, Father Baker and Brother Thomas were saying the Rosary. Suddenly Father Baker said,

"I don't know what's wrong, Brother, but I can't see. And my right eye pains me."

Brother Thomas suggested that he go to an eye specialist immediately to have an examination made, and that another priest be asked to say the Requiem Mass. But Father Baker would not do that, and continued on his way to Mt. St. Joseph.

After the Mass, he returned immediately to Our Lady of Victory Homes, and an eye specialist was called. After a thorough examination, the doctor told Father Baker that the eye was badly infected. Then, after a few days of careful watching of the eye, the doctor told him that it must be removed.

"Is it that bad?"

"Yes. The operation must be performed immediately, or your life is in danger."

Father Baker smiled. "My life is almost finished, Doctor. I am an old man, so we will not have the operation. It will be too much for everybody."

Everyone protested at this, and finally Father Baker said, "Well, it must be God's will that this should happen, and so I will have the operation when you are ready, Doctor."

One of Father Baker's customs was to keep a statue of Our Lady of Victory with him wherever he might be. When he went on a trip, the statue was the last item packed into his bag and the first one out of it. He would put it on the dresser in his room, wherever he might be, and then he was at home again.

As he grew older, it seemed that he wanted the statue of Our Lady of Victory with him all the time. Even when he went to bed at night, he would cradle it in his arm as he fell asleep, just as a little child might do with a favorite toy. It was symbolic, in a sense, for Father Baker's faith in Our Lady of Victory and her intercession with her divine Son was childlike in its intensity, in its wholehearted trust. He walked with Our Lady of Victory as a child walks with his mother, secure in the knowledge that his trust was not misplaced, and that he would be safeguarded from all harm.

This same faith accompanied him as he went to the operating room in Our Lady of Victory Hospital. The statue was cradled in his arms there, too, until the anesthetic made him unconscious, and when his arms relaxed the statue toppled to the floor.

Some of the hospital attendants were more concerned about Father Baker's reaction to the breaking of the statue than they were about the result of the operation. They were confident that Our Lady of Victory would ensure a successful operation, but would Father Baker be too upset over the broken statue? As a result, they picked up the pieces and hurried them over to one of the Brothers who repaired statues. When Father Baker came out of the anesthetic, the statue was waiting for him.

The operation was a success and, oddly enough, his left eye, which had been the weaker of the two, now strengthened as though his beloved Lady of Victory had obtained this favor for him.

The doctor warned Father Baker that he must be careful of his left eye. "Father," he said solemnly, "there are three important B's in your life — Boys, Babies, and Business. The first two are good for you; the third is not." But Father Baker resumed his regular business activities, and Brother Stanislaus had to remind him to take it easy.

"I'm all right, Brother," said Father Baker. "I don't know why God saw fit to send this cross and take my good eye, but if He wants the other one, He can have it."

A few years later, the dire effects of the great depression began to be felt in Lackawanna, in northern New York State, throughout the entire country. No one would have blamed Father Baker if he had left the solution of the problems arising out of it to others. A man then ninety years old, with only one eye, and subject certainly to some of the general infirmities of that age, could hardly be expected, practically

109

singlehandedly, to try to offset the starvation, the homelessness, the nakedness, the sickness that followed the black tide of depression. No one could have expected Father Baker to do this — no one, that is, but Father Baker. Where anyone was in need, Father Baker felt the obligation to help — and help he did, as his charity rose to undreamed-of heights.

Statistics do not tell the whole story, of course. But they are revealing of the extent of Father Baker's generous help to the needy, hungry, and homeless during those dark days. Unfortunately, shortly after Father Baker's death in 1936, the records at Our Lady of Victory's institutions were destroyed through some tragic mishap, and nothing remains there to indicate the scope of his generosity.

However, in the Buffalo chancery office files is a report, apparently prepared for the Bishop by Father Baker. It gives only a part of the story — from September 20, 1930, to early 1933 — and there are many indications that it is not all-inclusive. However, it is singularly revealing of how much Father Baker did for these needy ones, even though his own income had been severely limited by the stringent effects of the depression throughout the world.

From the period of September 20, 1930, to February 20, 1933, a total of 454,676 meals were served to the poor and needy. During the latter part of 1930, the number was relatively small, but by 1931 the number served each month doubled and tripled, until by September, 1931, more than 20,000 meals were being served to the hungry men who came to Father Baker's, hoping for food, and knowing in their hearts that they would not be turned away. The number continued to grow. By the summer of 1932, Father Baker was serving more than 30,000 meals a month to these poor people.

In a letter to Bishop Turner on April 17, 1931, Father Baker wrote: "We are still feeding the poor unemployed and the number still increases; since January 1, 1931, our daily feeding has been from 140 to 429 men, making a total of 24,400 meals during that time. . . . Our young shoemakers have put soles and heels on 2,189 pairs of shoes and have patched 389 pairs, which was a pleasure for them to do. The report for the Working Boys' Home shows that we have fed 140 men daily during the same time and have given 5,378 meals; the spare beds have been filled nightly. Our total expense has been over $3,000, but Our Lord has reimbursed us with over $10,000 to meet the expense. We find it very difficult to outdo our generous and beloved Lord."

In another report to the Bishop, Father Baker estimated that more than $50,000 had been spent from September 12, 1930, to August 31, 1933, to aid the poor and needy who came to him for assistance. Included in this was more than $5,600 which he noted as: "Total amount expended for rent of families in the neighborhood who could not pay their rent and which we had to guarantee and expend."

Those are the statistics, such as are available; and they do tell a tremendous story. But the human side of the story is more revealing, more indicative of Father Baker's approach to such a tragic situation in the lives of human beings.

His influence was powerful, and more than one time he used it to help individuals who were having difficulties, and at least once to help the entire community of Lackawanna.

During the very darkest days of the depression, the story goes, a rumor spread that there would be a "run" on the local bank, with all the people drawing out the money they had on deposit. Such a run is dangerous to any bank at any time; during the depression days it was doubly dangerous, and could be fatal for the bank.

Father Baker heard about this and very quickly took steps to kill the rumor. One day, when a large number of people were on the streets, he drove down to the bank with the entire Sunday collection and deposited it. Thus, in a very practical way, he showed his confidence in the bank and "saved" it. For, as people said, if Father Baker has confidence in it, it must be all right.

Another time Father Baker took a different approach with

a local bank. An elderly woman came to him in tears one night. She was behind in the interest payments on the mortgage which the bank held on her house. The bank had written her a sharp letter, saying that if the interest was not paid in full, they would have to foreclose the mortgage and take her house. Father Baker told her softly, "Don't worry about this. I'll go down to the bank in the morning, and everything will be all right."

He did go down to the bank in the morning, and told the manager forthrightly: "I don't think the bank will go out of business if you give that poor woman a little more time on her interest payments." And, due to Father Baker's intercession, the bank took a more lenient attitude, and she was able to keep her house.

The full story of the depression, and Father Baker's care of the people who came to him, probably can never be told. Who can measure how a hungry man is helped when he is given a warm meal? Or a family when a load of coal is delivered to heat a cold house? Father Baker did so many things that affected so many people in so many ways that it would be impossible to measure what might have been accomplished.

When the depression began and its effects became visible in the hunger of people, they came to Father Baker for food. He began by furnishing them bread, two and three loaves at a time, to take home for their families. Then, as the need became greater, he began asking the bakers in the surrounding area to donate day-old bread to him. As time went on, he began buying this day-old bread to satisfy the hunger of the people.

Soon the bread alone was not enough, and Father Baker set up a soup kitchen in the old Protectory building. Sometimes the line of hungry people would wind along for a block, as they waited to go into the kitchen and get a plate of heavy stew and all the bread they could eat. They would walk out into the yard and eat it in the sun, or sit on the benches in the rooms set aside for them.

112

If the people had shoes that needed repairing, they were sent down to the shoe shop. There the boys learning the shoe-maker trade would repair them. If the shoes were too badly worn, Father Baker had available repaired shoes which they could have. The men would look for their size, and walk out with a good-soled pair of shoes on their feet.

Many a man and woman — and children too — during those days were outfitted in fresh clothing by Father Baker. Accord-ing to the report filed with the diocesan chancery office, dur-ing the period from September 20, 1930, to January 7, 1933, 1500 men's shirts were given to the unemployed, 1825 pair of men's shoes, 1275 overcoats, 800 topcoats, and comparable amounts in women's and children's clothing.

Many too were housed through Father Baker's generosity. He set up some lodginghouses for men and women, so that they might have a place to sleep. There were, unfortunately, some unpleasant consequences in the matter of the lodging-houses for the men. Some of them were floaters and drifters, who had heard that there was free food and lodging at Father Baker's, and they came to take advantage of his kindness. He put these men up in some of the houses in Lackawanna, but they proved to be such unbearable neighbors that residents in the adjoining houses complained to the police.

The local authorities came to Father Baker with the com-plaints, but he tried to shrug them off. "Don't worry," he said. "They are all right."

"The people are complaining," said the police. "The men are filthy, and you'll have the state board of health down here."

"Don't worry," Father Baker repeated. "Everything will be all right."

But it wasn't, and the next day the mayor and the chief of police came to see Father Baker. "We don't like to go against you, Father, but those men have to get out of those houses. If they aren't out by noon, we'll arrest them all."

Father Baker looked at both of them, realizing that they

were intensely serious, and then said, "All right. They will be out." He had a truck take the men to the Working Boys' Home in Buffalo, where the Brothers of the Holy Infancy would be able to watch over them. And every day food was sent down to them from Lackawanna.

The men used to go across the street to the Buffalo city hall and sit on the steps, but their conduct had not improved. The police went over to inspect the Working Boys' Home and found that the men had gotten it in a filthy condition. So the next callers on Father Baker were the Buffalo city authorities. "We'll have to close that home if you don't get those men out of there," they told Father Baker. "The place is filthy; the men aren't using the toilets, and we cannot let that condition go on."

"They are my guests," Father Baker told the city authorities, "and that is my property."

But the Buffalo men retorted, "When they walk across the street and sit on the steps of city hall, they are vagrants. We will arrest them and, if we have to, close the Working Boys' Home."

Reluctantly, and only because he realized the authorities were right in the stand they had taken, Father Baker had the men moved out of the Working Boys' Home.

But instances such as these were very few; and there were bound to be some who would try to take advantage of a man like Father Baker. His attitude on that was reflected in another incident which happened about the same time.

Each evening, Father Baker would give out money to the people in need. They would line up and go into the Protectory building where he would stand at the head of the stairs, by his office, and give them a quarter or a half dollar as the need might be. This was enough to provide them with a bed for the night. Not unnaturally, some got into line twice, and one of Father Baker's assistants noticed that. "Father," he said, "some of these people are going to the end of the line, and coming through again, to get some more money."

114

"That's all right," said Father Baker quietly.

"But it isn't all right!" the other insisted. "Some of these people come up here in fancy cars to get bread and food and money — and they don't really need it."

"That's all right," Father Baker repeated. "When I die, our Lord isn't going to ask me if they were worthy. But He might ask me if I gave."

CHAPTER XV

FATHER BAKER'S generosity attracted thousands of homeless people to Lackawanna, as word spread of this priest who
gave food and clothing and even financial help to those who
needed it — and asked no questions.

Among these were many colored people from the South,
as well as from the Lackawanna and Buffalo area and different
parts of the North. Many of them were in desperate need;
many had met with prejudice in other localities when they
sought help, and it was a warming feeling for them to be
treated just like everyone else, as they were at Father Baker's.

As a result of this kindness one of the Negroes wanted to
become a Catholic so he asked a Brother in the kitchen how
to go about it. Some of the others also said they wanted to
know more about this religion of Father Baker's that made
him help so many people.

The Brother, of course, brought this word to Father Baker,
who quickly realized the tremendous opportunity that was
being presented to him. He called one of his assistants and
outlined his plans, prefacing it thus:

"I was talking to a missionary from China one day. He
had been in China for six years. How many converts do you
think he had?" Without waiting for the assistant to reply,
Father Baker said: "He didn't have fifty in six years.

"I remember years ago talking to another missionary," he
continued. "He had one convert in a whole year — a whole

year of working among the people in his territory. But we have a wonderful apostolate here at home. There are hundreds and hundreds of colored people that we don't have to go out to reach. They are right at our door. They are asking for instruction in the Church. Some of them have talked to Brother and are asking to know more about our religion. I want you to go down and teach them."

"When would this be, Father?"

"Every afternoon at four o'clock."

"Every afternoon?"

"Oh, yes. It would have to be every afternoon."

The assistant shook his head slowly. "If that's what you want me to do, of course I'll do it. But I don't know if it is physically possible unless some of my other duties are taken away. I hear confessions five days a week, and then help take care of the orphanage, the grammar school, and the high school. Still, if you say so, I'll do the best I can."

"Fine," said Father Baker. "We'll let you know."

However, recognizing the burden of work carried by his assistants, Father Baker decided to make other arrangements, and secured the services of Father Thomas Galvin, a Redemptorist priest who had been a "Father Baker boy" and had now retired. Each day Father Galvin came out to Lackawanna from Buffalo and gave instructions to the Negroes, who crowded into a converted classroom to learn about the Catholic Church. Later another diocesan priest was sent to Father Baker's institutions to assist him, and he was immediately assigned to work with the Negroes.

This was during 1933, 1934, and 1935, when Father Baker was 91, 92, or 93, and when one might expect he would be less alert. But his assistants recall that even at that age, he was very shrewd and very acute. As one remarked, "He seemed to know what we were doing and where we were going and what work we had under way."

Almost every afternoon Father Baker would be down in the classroom, while the instructions were being given to the

Negroes. Before that, he would have put in a full day in the office. As one assistant there during that time remarked, "For a person of that age and the general debility of that age, it would seem incredible that he could do things like that."

After the instructions, the people would go into another room, where they would have soup and bread. Afterward they would go upstairs, and Father Baker with some of his assistants would be standing at the head of the stairs, near his office in the Protectory Building. Almost every day Father Baker would take a pocketful of dimes and quarters — probably $25 to $30 worth — and give them out to the needy people as they came up the stairs.

Here again, as so frequently happened with his works of charity, Father Baker was criticized. One assistant recalls someone saying to him: "Father Baker, some of these people are not worthy. You are giving away this money, and you don't know anything about these people. There is bound to be someone who isn't worthy of your help. Why should you waste your money on them?"

Father Baker turned to face the questioner, with his one good eye and his one bad eye, and asked simply, "Which one is not worthy?"

There were always those who came out to see what Father Baker was doing and could not refrain from giving him advice. To one who voiced the same criticism as above, Father Baker said, "I would rather give to nine unworthy ones than to deprive one who is worthy."

Sometimes these self-appointed critics — well meaning as they were — would press their point. Then Father Baker would resort to this comment, which was as sharp as he would ever get with anyone: "Mind your own business."

His Negro apostolate received its share of criticism. He held the classes for them every afternoon, but some felt that the Negro converts were not receiving sufficient instructions. One assistant there during the period of the Negro apostolate said he thought, at the time, that diocesan regulations called for twenty periods of instruction, and the Negro converts received the required number. However, these were given daily, rather than once a week, as is often done in parish work.

One monsignor from New York City, who had a large Negro parish, came to see Father Baker's work. He inquired about the period of instructions given to the Negro converts, and then said, as though disparaging the fact that instructions were given daily: "We would never accept Negro converts in less than two years of instructions."

Father Baker's comment was like a two-edged sword, as he asked in his soft, quiet manner: "How long a time do you give a white person instructions?"

Father Baker had an uncanny knack of making comments like that, softly, gently, usually in the form of a question — but one that was unanswerable . . . as, for instance, the time he answered another individual by saying, "Did St. Francis Xavier give all those people over in India a full course of instruction before he baptized them?"

During the years, a neighboring parish, St. Charles Borromeo, had faded out of existence. The old church had been torn down and Victory Hall built in its place. Father Baker decided, "As long as we have this beautiful new building and it has a nice auditorium, it will be the chapel for the colored people." Using a little basin as a temporary baptismal font, Father Baker baptized the first class of converts there as they marched up in long white garments. Then, on the first Sunday after their baptism, they all received Holy Communion, and Father Baker, despite his age, preached the sermon.

Two incidents that happened during the Negro apostolate movement, as it might be called, show Father Baker's feelings toward the Negro. The police felt that Father Baker's charity was bringing a lot of undesirable people into Lackawanna, and rather naturally picked up a number of them and put them in jail.

Captain Rose, formerly in the Lackawanna Police Department and now retired, recalls that "Father Baker was very offended and sent for me. Of course I had to have some kind of story to tell him. I told him we picked up a Negro with a wooden leg, who came from Texas. He swore up and down that he didn't have any money, but when we took the leg off, we found some $80 stuffed way down in it. Of course that kind of pacified the thing."

Another time some of the Negroes coming into Lackawanna to see Father Baker were beaten up and run out of town, according to Margaret Bernardo, who had worked closely with Father Baker in the conversion of the Negroes. Some of them went and washed off the blood and then came to Father Baker and explained what had happened. In telling his helpers about it, Father Baker said, "Once before in my life I cried, but then I had two eyes. Now I have only one eye, but this morning when Dave and those men came and told me how they had been beaten and run away from here, I couldn't help crying again."

Another time, Mrs. Bernardo recalls, Father Baker was taking them through the beautiful Basilica, showing them everything, and he said, "Once I thought the only thing that could ever please me was when I built this Basilica. But this has pleased me more — to convert the Negroes to Jesus Christ, and I know it is a blessing."

He was completely generous, completely unselfish in his treatment of the Negro people, says one of the priests who worked with him at that time. "There was nothing of self-glory in it at all. It was strictly a spiritual act."

Father Baker's complete charity showed itself in another incident that concerned the Negro people. One night one of his assistants heard a noise out in the hall and opened his door to see a huge Negro man standing there. The man was probably frightened at the door opening so suddenly, so he just stood there and stared at the priest. The priest was so upset at the incident that he slammed the door.

However, the next morning he was still angry at what had happened, and stormed in to see Father Baker.

120

"Father," he said sharply, "you've got to keep those Negroes out of here!"

"Who?" asked Father Baker, in his usual soft voice.

"Those Negroes! They are coming in and knocking on my door in the middle of the night." And then he told what had happened the night before.

"What did he want?" asked Father Baker.

"He was probably looking for a place to sleep," said the assistant priest.

"Why didn't you give him your bed?" asked Father Baker in that soft voice.

"You can give him yours if you want," the assistant replied tartly, "but if I see any more up there, I'll call the police."

Perhaps what upset the assistant most was that he knew, in his heart, that Father Baker would have given the man his own bed if there were no other sleeping place available for him.

A Jesuit priest, visiting Father Baker in 1934, asked, "How did you manage it all, Father? Where did you get the money?"

Father Baker's reply — as always — was to point to a statue of Our Lady of Victory. "I had very little to do with it. She did it all! The Blessed Mother is my manager, my banker. I am the administrator and I never worry."

And then he said, "Come and see my Negro converts. Two hundred have been baptized already, and Bishop Turner will confirm them next week."

The Jesuit tells how he left Father Baker there, teaching catechism to colored adults. And this was in his ninety-second year!

It is difficult to visualize the tremendous work that Father Baker did during his long lifetime of service to God and his fellow men. In 1935 he gave a talk in which he summarized the work of his institutions, and the talk took five typewritten pages of notes!

During the many years he had been at Lackawanna, these

are some of the institutions he managed and founded:

Two missions established in neighboring areas, with a school built at one and a church at the other.

The Working Boys' Home and two Working Girls' Homes in Buffalo. These were for older boys and girls who were working away from home, but were under Father Baker's care after working hours.

At Lackawanna:

St. Joseph's Orphan Asylum, which cared for about 200 boys during the year.

Our Lady of Victory Infant Home, which had cared for a total of 6500 infants and small children.

Our Lady of Victory Hospital, which cared for more than 3000 poor sick people during the year, many of whom "were too poor to pay anything."

St. John's Protectory, where "hundreds of homeless, abandoned, neglected, or wayward boys" were cared for during the years.

He had established trade schools at Lackawanna for the boys, where they learned tailoring, barbering, carpenter work, glazing, laundering, plumbing, electric work, shoe making and repairing, photography and sign painting, painting and printing.

Then there was the magnificent national shrine, the Basilica of Our Lady of Victory, to which thousands come each year.

What a monument Father Baker had built throughout the years, for the greater glory of God, and for and through the intercession of His Mother under her title of Our Lady of Victory!

CHAPTER XVI

IN 1936, Father Baker became seriously ill. He was then ninety-four years old, but he had recovered from so many serious illnesses it was hard to believe that this might be his last.

One of the newly ordained priests that year, Father Joseph M. McPherson, had been assigned to Our Lady of Victory Homes, and he came to the hospital to visit his new pastor. He knocked gently on the door, and then waited for the nurse to answer.

On this June day, Father Baker was feeling moderately well, though he had been ill since April. The nurse beckoned Father McPherson into the hospital room.

"Here's a nice young priest come to visit you," the nurse told the frail old man, whose slight body hardly weighed more than a hundred pounds.

Father Baker raised his head and looked at the young priest. Then he smiled weakly and said, "You're just as much a priest as I am. Will you give me your blessing, Father?"

Father McPherson would rather have received a blessing from Father Baker, but, greatly impressed by the humility shown by the request, he gave the saintly old man his blessing.

He was to be the last assistant appointed to aid Father Baker in his charitable works, probably the only assistant that Father Baker did not know was coming and whom he did not in fact select.

As vicar-general of the Buffalo diocese, Father Baker had an important hand in the assignment of priests, but during this spring and early summer of 1936, his health and his memory had been quite poor. He had started to slip noticeably in April, both physically and mentally; and from then on, except for occasional "good" days, his health deteriorated.

Father McPherson, like many of the boys and young men in the Buffalo area, had been familiar with the work of Father Baker. Perhaps he knew more than most, for he had been brought up by his brother-in-law, who sold furniture to the institutions. Father McPherson's brother-in-law would often go out to Lackawanna just for an excuse to talk to Father Baker, and that feeling of admiration and even reverence had been passed on to the young priest.

But even he had fallen victim to the threat of being sent to Father Baker's institutions. It was common among Buffalo families, non-Catholic as well as Catholic, to say to their youngsters, "If you're not good, I'll send you to Father Baker's." Many prominent men in that area recall today with a smile that they had their bags packed more than once, ready for an unwilling trip to Father Baker's institutions.

Now Father Baker was dying, as he had seemed to be for some months. Throughout Buffalo, throughout New York State, the United States, and Canada, countless friends and supporters of his work were praying for Father Baker.

His death was believed so imminent that Bishop Turner of Buffalo had prepared a funeral oration for the Requiem Mass. It was found among the Bishop's papers on his desk — for he died on July 10, 1936, while Father Baker still lived, though in very critical condition.

Father Baker's condition was so critical that he did not even know that Bishop Turner had died. On July 12, when the authorities of the diocese met to choose an administrator, it was necessary to summon Father Baker, as the senior monsignor of the diocese. The notification was handed to Father Baker, as required, but he was too weak to read it, and

124

he was not even told that Bishop Turner, his very good friend, had died.

In mid-July, Cardinal Pacelli, later to become Pope Pius XII, sent a cable to Monsignor Baker from the Vatican: "The Holy Father sends Your Reverence his affectionate apostolic benediction, invoking fortitude and divine comfort in your illness."

At 2 a.m. on July 29, Father Baker lapsed into a coma. He had received extreme unction on July 17, but life still lingered in his frail body until July 29, when death came at 9:20 a.m. Outside the door of Room 215 in Our Lady of Victory Hospital, which he had built years before, the Sisters of St. Joseph and the Brothers of the Holy Infancy were saying the prayers for the dying. Inside, priests of the diocese of Buffalo, Father Baker's assistants, doctors, and nurses watched and prayed. As Father Baker breathed his last, Rev. Joseph A. Burke of Kenmore, later to become the ninth Bishop of Buffalo, gave him the last blessing.

The news of Father Baker's death spread rapidly throughout the city. At the hospital switchboard, Sister St. Luke of the Sisters of St. Joseph closed each call with this message: "Father Baker died at 9:20 this morning. Now you pray for him."

The Buffalo newspapers brought out their biggest headlines, and used pages of stories and pictures to depict the tremendous achievements of this great man, whose charity and generosity had endeared him to thousands throughout the area. The *Buffalo Times* wrote editorially:

"To have known Father Baker was to marvel at his energy and at the works that flowed from it.

"Discount, as the incredulous will, the miracles that have become so firmly associated with the shrine he built to Our Lady of Victory, and examine the attested record of his achievement:

"To the hungry during his ministry he fed 50 million meals. During the depression at one time he was serving more than a million meals a year. He gave away a million loaves of bread. He clothed the naked to the number of a half million. He gave medical care to 250,000 and supplied medicines to 200,000 more. Three hundred thousand men, women, and children received some sort of education or training at his hands. A hundred thousand boys were trained for trades. Six hundred unmarried mothers in their distress knocked at his door and did not knock in vain. More than 6,000 destitute and abandoned babies were placed in foster homes. . . .

"And so passes a man whose greatness was not in stone, or eloquence, or statecraft, but in a compassionate heart. He will feel at home among the saints. And men will give thanks that he lived and bless his memory."

There is no question that many persons agreed with the *Buffalo Times* editorial. One priest stated later, "There is not the slightest shadow of a doubt that at that time everybody not only was convinced that he was a saint, but that he was going to be canonized some day."

Messages of condolence and sympathy came to the Buffalo diocesan officials from all over the world. A cablegram from Vatican City declared: "The Holy Father is deeply grieved to hear of the death of Msgr. Baker, the well-beloved American apostle of charity. He extends paternal sympathy to the bereaved diocese and assures his prayers for the repose of the soul of this faithful servant of his God and the poor."

As the messages of condolence came to Buffalo and Lackawanna from the great and the mighty, from the unknown and the poor, the body of Father Baker was prepared for its last resting place. He was to be buried, not in the Basilica of Our Lady of Victory, as many had supposed, but at his specific request in Holy Cross Cemetery. This was just across Ridge Road from Our Lady of Victory Hospital where he died, just a few feet from the many institutions he had founded for the helpless and the destitute, and alongside the bodies of his mother and father.

126

Because of the greatness of Father Baker's life, and perhaps, too, because of the many unusual cures — they are called "miracles" by some — which had been attributed to his prayers, exceptional care was taken during the embalming, funeral, and burial of Father Baker.

One of the young assistant priests at Our Lady of Victory institutions was instructed by the diocesan officials to stay with the embalmers, to see that nothing unusual was done. When the blood was removed, it was placed in permanent-type jars, and these were placed in the grave with the body of Father Baker.

Dressed in his robes as a Prothonotary Apostolic — a high honorary distinction which allowed Father Baker to wear some of the ceremonial ornaments of a bishop — the body was first placed in the nurses' home which Father Baker had built many years before. Men of the Lackawanna police and fire departments made up the guard of honor, followed by the Knights of St. John.

Then the body was moved to the Basilica of Our Lady of Victory, where it lay in state before the high altar — and thousands upon thousands, some from far distances, came to pay their last respects to this great man.

All through the day, and even through most of the night, they lined up, four abreast, across the street from the Basilica. And then the line moved slowly down Ridge Road toward the cemetery gates, almost a half mile away, where the people crossed the street and moved slowly back to the Basilica of Our Lady of Victory.

The line lasted until two or three o'clock each morning, and then, very early, it would start again. People came from all over the United States and from Canada, whole families with even small children, to pay their last respects to Father Baker.

Many of them had been "Father Baker boys," who had been sheltered by him when they were small, who had grown up in his institutions, had learned a trade, and then moved

127

away and established their own homes and their own families. Others had aided his charitable work and been aided by his prayers.

Estimates of the number of people who viewed Father Baker's body as it lay in state varied only in actual numbers; everyone agreed that it ran to the hundreds of thousands. Some estimates went as high as 500,000 persons; others said at least 300,000.

The police of Lackawanna said that at times around 92 persons a minute were passing the casket in the great Basilica. At all times a guard of honor was around the casket, and in many ways it was not only a guard of honor. It was an actual guard, and very much needed, as those with a deep and fervent devotion to Father Baker and his tremendous works tried to take "souvenirs" as they passed his casket.

Shortly after the body was removed to the shrine of Our Lady of Victory from the nurses' home, one woman attempted to snip a lock of hair from Father Baker's head, presumably hoping to secure a "relic" for herself. There were also reports that some people had attempted to cut off pieces of his vestments, as he lay in the casket.

One point is definite, however, and showed the great affection and admiration in which Father Baker was held by all those who came to pray for his soul in the days before his funeral. Because he was a Prothonotary Apostolic of the Church, Father Baker's hands had been dressed with white gloves. Those who came to view his body had been warned not to touch the body or his clothing. But they did — with rosaries, medals, with all kinds of religious articles. And so many of these visitors touched Father Baker's hands that they finally wore through the gloves.

CHAPTER **XVII**

THE seemingly never ending line of mourners started at the corner of South Park Avenue and Ridge Road in Lackawanna. The people walked four abreast, almost as though in procession, down Ridge Road.

As they did so, the wonderful works of Father Baker passed in review before their eyes, almost as a panorama of his amazing achievements, through his faith in God, his never failing trust in Our Lady of Victory — and his unswerving devotion to the little ones of God, to the poor and the helpless people of the world.

The corner of South Park and Ridge Road was familiar to many of the viewers. Many had come there as children with their parents, to attend the closing of the novenas which Father Baker had made so famous. The small St. Patrick's Church, which stood on the site of the present Basilica, was much too small for those crowded ceremonies. They had come by trolley car from Buffalo, or by the railroad trains, or by horse and buggy.

Here too Father Baker had held the lawn fetes and the other social affairs that had helped to raise money for his ever growing charitable institutions. One of Father Baker's friends tells this story about one of the benefit barbecues during Father Baker's later years, after he had lost one eye.

"As we neared the pavilion, I noticed some men working on beer barrels and putting up wheels of chance. Father Baker noticed this too. But he could only see out of one eye, and not too well at that. He suggested that we go closer and see what was going on.

"The men at the beer barrels motioned violently to me to keep Father Baker away — but once Father Baker started on something, he was hard to stop. He went over to the pavilion, squinted at the beer barrels, and asked the workers, 'What have we here?'

" 'Why — why, these are the ice-cream machines, Father,' one of the embarrassed men said.

" 'Oh,' said Father Baker. Then he looked up quizzically and said, 'Those are the funniest looking ice-cream machines I ever saw.' "

Next to this open place stood St. Joseph's Orphan Asylum, one of the first buildings. Then came the lovely wayside shrine to Our Lady of Victory, which had been erected first on the site of the present basilica. Many who had prayed frequently at the shrine could almost recall word for word the inscription there:

"This lovely little shrine is the original shrine of Our Lady of Victory, erected by Father Baker. When completed in May, 1894, it stood on the site of the present basilica and was moved here when construction began. Father Baker, who spent virtually all of his 60 priestly years with the boys and babies here (1876–1936), was accustomed to visit this shrine each day. Over the years it has become a favorite spot for pilgrims to kneel in prayer and to take a picture as a memento of their visit."

The next building in Father Baker's "row" of institutions was the Infant Home, which he established to care for unmarried mothers and their children.

Then, between the Infant Home and the Hospital, was the place that many, many years ago used to be called Father Baker's "prayer path" — and, later, "Father Baker's folly." This is where he decided to drill for gas, at the end of the walk he used when he read his breviary each day.

130

Then came Our Lady of Victory Hospital, which Father Baker had first intended only as a hospital for the unwed mothers and their children, but which has become a vast general hospital, doing untold good for the community and the neighboring areas.

The line of mourners for Father Baker continued down the road to the cemetery, crossed over, and then continued back along Ridge Road toward the Basilica. It passed old St. John's Protectory, the original building to which Father Baker added so much. Some of the mourners would recall the heavy metal screens that used to be on the windows — to keep the boys in — and which Father Baker took down.

They would recall, too, the "yard" behind the building, where the boys had their games, and where they greeted Father Baker with cheers and flocked about him as he came down to visit with them.

As the line worked its way into the Basilica, toward the solid bronze casket, many carried rosaries and other religious articles, which they touched to the body of the man they loved and respected. Many too threw coins and medals into the casket, which is more a foreign than an American custom. But Lackawanna was a city of almost 60 different nationalities, and Father Baker had helped all of them.

Among the persons who streamed through the Basilica during those days of mourning was a young steelworker of Lackawanna who had a lot of faith in Father Baker. He had an accident at the steel plant, and his right arm had been ripped open. Every tendon, every muscle was cut in half. He had no movement in his arm. For a year and a half, he couldn't move a muscle from his fingers to his shoulder. He had been told that he would never move the arm by its own power.

Every night, while Father Baker's body lay in state, he had walked in the long line, down one side of Ridge Road and up the other, to have a few precious seconds near the casket in the Basilica. And each time, with his left hand, he lifted

131

up his right arm, in its heavy cast, and placed it on Father Baker's body lying in the solid bronze casket. And he prayed that something would happen to repair his damaged arm.

Father Baker was buried in Holy Cross Cemetery. Nothing happened, but the steelworker prayed on. A few nights later, while he was asleep, at about three or four o'clock in the morning, his right arm suddenly swung over in a huge arc, hit his wife, lying beside him, and gave her a black eye. She woke up and screamed: "Tom! Tom! You moved your arm!"

The cast has been off for years now; he has full motion in his arm and in his hand and fingers. The only evidence of the accident is an ugly scar running along the inside of his arm. The file on his accident is still open at the steel plant. They have never closed it, thinking that something might happen later on to make the tendons or the muscles shrink. "Thank God," the steelworker says today, "I never had to go back and open that. My arm is just as good today as it was 23 years ago. And there is only one person I give credit to — Father Baker."

The funeral of Father Baker was held on August 3, 1936. A crowd estimated at 25,000 persons gathered about the Basilica of Our Lady of Victory for the Pontifical Requiem Mass, which was said by Father Baker's long-time friend, Bishop Walsh of Newark. One of Father Baker's treasured mementoes was an autographed picture of Bishop Walsh, which hung in his private chapel. It was inscribed: "To my dear and true friend, the Rt. Rev. Msgr. Nelson H. Baker, with my love, admiration, prayers and best wishes."

The day of the funeral, the Basilica was packed with priests, Brothers, and Sisters, and with those members of the laity who were able to stand inside the doors. Outside, the streets were jammed. One of the policemen on duty there said, "On the morning of the funeral we had to keep the street open; we had to preserve a fire lane. The place was packed — I couldn't see how far. You couldn't get anywhere near the corner."

132

The eulogy was preached by Most Rev. Thomas F. Hickey, former Bishop of Rochester, New York, and then the titular Archbishop of Viminacium. "The Church today mourns one of God's most devoted priests," the Archbishop declared at the conclusion of the Mass. "His faith was that of the true follower of Christ. All through life the beauty and simplicity of his faith stand out. In his hope and trust, he knew no limit to place in the trust he had for God. His whole life was the love of God. Everything he did was for the love of God and God's creatures. Father Baker's humility touches all those virtues.

"He was always first an instrument in the hands of God. His work was for the love of God and God's children. Father Baker was like St. Alphonsus, for he loved Christ and his soul burned with the desire to give souls to Christ.

"Father Baker's works were extraordinary and incredible. Valuable, far-reaching though they may be, I prefer to take his soul, and his life, which he gave to Christ. The value of his life was his holiness. . . .

"Dear Father Baker, you have heard the word of the true Christ. Your heart has been in the tabernacle and at the foot of the cross. Christ now is ready to give you the treasures of heaven for eternity, and so we say 'Eternal rest grant to him, oh Lord, and let perpetual light shine upon him.'"

Bishop Walsh then gave the last blessing, and the casket was sealed. In it was a statue of Our Lady of Victory, a portrait of his mother, the late Caroline M. Baker, and her gold wedding ring. The statue was the one which had fallen and broken when Father Baker had his eye removed.

What might be called unusual precautions were made in regard to Father Baker's grave. There was actually a cement vault built into the ordinary grave and then sealed by .the Church authorities.

A few days after the funeral, Father Baker's will was filed in Surrogate's Court in Buffalo. It is a most amazing document, especially when one realizes that this is the will of a

133

man who handled millions of dollars during his lifetime. He died at an age far beyond that of most men, and certainly with his financial acuteness and the possibilities for savings and investments available to him, it is a most revealing document of his character and his lack of self-centeredness.

The will, made on July 7, 1922, read as follows:

"In the name of the Father and of the Son and of the Holy Ghost. Amen.

"I, Nelson H. Baker, being of sound mind and body, do hereby declare this to be my last will and testament:

"First — I have no money in any bank, no bonds nor securities of any kind or form; and I am indebted to no one financially, and no one is indebted to me.

"There is no salary due me from the Diocese of Buffalo, St. John's Protectory, St. Joseph's Male Orphan Asylum, the Society for the Protection of Destitute Roman Catholic Children at the City of Buffalo, Our Lady of Victory Infant Home, the Working Boys' Home, Association of Our Lady of Victory, or any other institution of which I have had charge, or from the parish of which I have been rector.

"I have no property of any kind, except certain chattels donated to me by kind friends during my life, such as books, altar furniture, certain articles of furniture, clothing, etc.; and I wish the institutions which have been under my charge in Lackawanna, hereinafter named, to have these. Therefore, I give to Ass'n of Our Lady of Victory, a corporation created under the laws of the state of New York, to take gifts by devise, bequest and otherwise and collect funds for the charitable work done at St. John's Protectory and St. Joseph's Male Orphan Asylum, in what is now the city of Lackawanna, any property I may have at my death.

"Second — I wish to thank my friends for their great and continued kindness to me and to the work entrusted to my care; and I earnestly request their prayers. I place my soul in the hands of Our Blessed Savior and our dear Blessed Lady of Victory, and hope we will meet again in heaven, never to be separated.

"Third — I appoint my friend and legal counselor, Charles Leo O'Connor, to be the executor of this, my last will and testament; and I hereby revoke any wills heretofore made by me."

Father Baker added three codicils to this remarkable will. The first, dated January 11, 1928, read:

"I, Nelson H. Baker, with unfaltering trust in God, hereby making public expression of my gratitude to Him for the manifold blessings which he has showered upon me during my life, and professing my faith in the doctrines of the Roman Catholic Church to which, in His goodness, He has called me to be a priest, and acknowledging all those favors, and especially the marvelous gifts He has bestowed through the intercession of Our Blessed Lady of Victory, do hereby declare this to be a codicil to my last will and testament, which bears date the seventh day of July, in the year of Our Lord, One Thousand Nine Hundred and Twenty-Two."

The second codicil was dated only a year before his death, on June 19, 1935. In it Father Baker paid high tribute to the Sisters of St. Joseph as he wrote:

"The Sisters of St. Joseph long have had faithful and devoted charge of Our Lady of Victory hospital, Lackawanna, N. Y., and they have long since added a dispensary and clinic to the work, which has increased their capacity, and they have cared for hundreds of poor people troubled with all kinds of diseases, without charge, and we have been benefited in this way, and Our Most Reverend Bishop and myself would like to have this class of work continued by the good Sisters of St. Joseph who have made so many sacrifices to assist those in need.

"We would not like this to be discontinued or interfered with in any way, as we know that Our Lord will bless us for the good that the Sisters are continuing to do in Our

Lady of Victory hospital, and that Our Lord will continue to bless us as long as this work is continued."

The third codicil, dated five days later on June 24, 1935, ratified and confirmed the provisions previously made.

Thus ended the career of a great and generous and even saintly man, who had aided thousands upon thousands during the ninety-four years of his busy and productive life. Thus ended a life which had begun on February 16, 1842, in the then small town of Buffalo.

CHAPTER XVIII

THAT was nearly twenty-five years ago — and yet the memory of Father Baker and his good works live on. Each year, on the anniversary of his death, thousands of people come to Our Lady of Victory's shrine in Lackawanna, to join in prayers for this great and generous man who lived to serve God's poor coming to him for assistance from all over the world.

Almost every Sunday, too, if you visit his grave in Holy Cross Cemetery, you will see people kneeling there to pray — for the repose of his soul and for his help in solving their problems. Some of them seem like little problems — but they are important to these troubled people, and Father Baker helps them. Some of them are very serious problems — and Father Baker helps there too.

Sometimes these are Father Baker's boys, whose memory still recalls the slender priest who greeted them so gaily, who sustained them when they had been orphaned, who gave them a training in a trade so they could earn their living when they became older. Sometimes they are men and women who have participated in Father Baker's novenas, who have gained some favor through his help, through Our Lady of Victory's intercession.

None of them have forgotten Father Baker. When you talk to them and ask about Father Baker, their eyes light up and they talk about him so vividly that you almost expect him to walk into the room. His earthly life ended in 1936, but his spirit lives in the memories of all those whom he helped through his long life on this earth.

And they all, it seems, have some interesting anecdote, some unusual cure that they attribute to Father Baker and his beloved Lady of Victory — as, for instance, the mother who was to have a gall-bladder operation. She had been sick for weeks, and finally the doctor sent her to the hospital. All of the preliminary tests had been taken, and she was ready to be wheeled into the operating room when she balked, because, she said, "My baby then was seven months old, and I didn't want to leave her. So I told the doctor, I am going home and pray to Father Baker for a miracle."

The doctor was a little bit provoked after getting her all ready, but he said, "While you're at it, pray for me too."

"Doctor," she said, "I am going to be pretty busy praying for my own. If you have anything to pray for, you better pray yourself."

She went home and started to pray and has never had any such attacks since. And that was eighteen years ago.

A Jewish businessman near Buffalo has a picture of Father Baker in a prominent place in his office. "I wouldn't even have this business," he says, "if it weren't for Father Baker."

He once had a partnership in Buffalo, and one day the partner walked out, taking all the firm's assets. He had nothing left, and he didn't know where to turn. Somehow he was led to Father Baker. "Have faith in Our Lady of Victory, and everything will be fine," Father Baker told him. And everything was fine.

"I am a Jew," the man says now. "I am not a Catholic. But there was something godly and superhuman about Father Baker. He was a living saint if there ever was one. I don't pass a day but, in my own little way, I say a prayer of thanksgiving to him for putting me in the wonderful situation I am in today."

Another story concerns a retired policeman in Lackawanna

138

who had lost a great deal of weight and was down to 123 pounds — and this police lieutenant is now a big man. They brought him to Our Lady of Victory Hospital for an operation. After the doctors operated, they just sewed him up again. They knew that they could do nothing for him. They said he was full of cancer, and that he was dying. The lieutenant himself knew it, and this is what he says about it now:

"I was dying. I know that I was, and I was told by all that I didn't have a chance. They told my wife to be prepared — that I couldn't live for ten minutes.

"The Sisters at the hospital were saying the prayers for the dying for me. I had a fever of about 107, they told me. Then one of the Sisters got a cross that belonged to Father Baker. They said I used to help them across the street at the hospital — and now they were going to help me.

"When I took hold of that cross, I felt like something or someone gripped my hand, and it seemed to lift me up. Within a month or so I was out of the hospital.

"The doctor said I wouldn't live for six months. At the end of six months, I went back to him and he said, you'll never live for five years. At the end of five years, I went back again and said, 'Doctor, the five years are up.' And that was about fifteen years ago. I couldn't speak for the two doctors, but everyone else says it was a miracle."

No one knows, of course, whether it was a miracle. It certainly was an unusual cure, and not an unprecedented one. All through Father Baker's life people were cured of ailments — to whom, perhaps, Father Baker said, "Don't worry — you'll be all right." And they were.

Another man says his wife was very sick. Three doctors had been called in consultation, and their decision was unanimous — they would have to operate. Father Baker came down one evening to visit the sick woman and blessed her with a relic. Two or three days later the doctors came to make a final check before the operation. The family doctor, a non-Catholic, told the husband, "There has been a miracle here." And no operation was necessary.

There are other stories about Father Baker that show his kindness, his humor, and his gentleness with everyone.

A former policeman tells about an old woman who used to come out to Holy Cross Cemetery on Sundays to sell peanuts at the gate. Some businessmen in town complained about it. They wanted the policeman to chase the old woman away, but he said, "I'll see Father Baker first before I do anything about it."

Father Baker just laughed. "Poor old woman," he told the policeman. "She comes out only on Sunday afternoon to make a few dollars, but the businessmen have all week to do their business. I'm not going to tell you to chase her off my property." And the policeman didn't, as he told the businessmen.

This same policeman tells about a man caught robbing the poor box at Our Lady of Victory shrine. He was taken to the police station, to face trial in the morning. Father Baker heard about it — as he did about most things that happened in Lackawanna and Buffalo — and sent word to the police, asking them to let the man go. "If he didn't need the money," Father Baker said, "he wouldn't have taken it."

Father Baker was known to do these little kindnesses every day, and as a matter of course. He would see a new boy in the yard, off by himself, fighting homesickness, and he would go over, talk to the boy, tell him a funny story or two — or just have the boy walk around the yard with him. Soon the boy would be feeling better, and his whole outlook on life would change.

Or Father Baker might let some of the older boys go into Buffalo to see a new movie. Before they left, he would ask, "Do you have enough money?" Often he would press a bill into the hands of one and say, "Take a little extra along. You might need it."

He trusted the boys, as a parent trusts his sons — and he

140

was a true father to the thousands of boys given into his care. Many of them, who came to Father Baker with nothing, left with the feeling that someone cared for them, that someone trusted them — and they lived up to that trust.

Father Baker left many monuments that will endure as long as memories last — the magnificent buildings he erected which form a little city of their own, a "holy city," which dominates one section of Lackawanna and irresistibly draws thousands to it every year.

He left monuments, too, in the hearts and minds of thousands of boys who are the better for having known him, whose faith and spirit had grown under his care. These may prove to be the more enduring — but certainly Father Baker laid up for himself treasures in heaven, treasures that will last for all eternity.

In the minds of thousands he built an everlasting devotion to his beloved Lady of Victory, who was his "banker," as he often said, and for whom he was only the "administrator — she did all the work." And now we hope, with him, as he expressed the hope in his last will and testament, that he has met with our Lord and Our Lady of Victory, in heaven, "never to be separated" from them.

EPILOGUE

WHAT has happened in the years since Father Baker's death in 1936? So often, as someone has said, an institution is but the lengthened shadow of a man. Certainly Our Lady of Victory Homes of Charity is a living manifestation of the tremendous work of Father Baker, as Monsignor Joseph M. McPherson, the present superintendent, would be the first to insist. It is more; it is a living manifestation of the protecting hand of Our Lady of Victory, still shielding the institutions named after her; still sustaining them through the generous offerings of her clients all over the world.

A little example will show this. You will remember the gas well which Father Baker drilled against much opposition, and in which he persisted, even when the drillers felt he was throwing away the money which belonged, they felt, to the care of the children. The gas well came in, unexpectedly and strongly, so that many called it Father Baker's "miraculous" gas well.

That was way back in 1891. And the gas well is still producing gas for the institutions of Our Lady of Victory in Lackawanna. It has never failed to provide the needed gas, to the amazement of many experts. With the growth of the hospital and the other buildings, this natural gas now is used primarily for the cooking and hot-water needs of all the homes. Sometimes experts will hazard guesses as to where the gas comes from; and Monsignor McPherson might be quoting Father Baker's own words as he says, "I don't really care where Our Lady of Victory finds the gas, so long as she keeps providing it for her institutions here."

142

In this devotion to Our Lady of Victory, Monsignor McPherson is also reflecting the devotion of her many clients who through the years have continued their aid to the Homes. This is shown in the many pilgrimages each year that visit the Basilica of Our Lady of Victory and the Our Lady of Victory Homes of Charity; the fervent interest in the novena devotions which were started by Father Baker when he first came to Lackawanna; and the continued membership in the Association of Our Lady of Victory, which was Father Baker's first public promotion of his beloved heavenly advocate.

There is much at Lackawanna that is the same as it was during the latter years of Father Baker's life; there are changes, too, just as Father Baker would have made changes to "keep up with the times." Father Baker was never one to be behind times; his alert mind kept him usually ahead of the times, rather than merely abreast of them. And so Our Lady of Victory Homes of Charity keep up with the times — and sometimes break new trails in the care of the needy, the young, the suffering.

The Infant Home, for instance, still maintains the same three phases as established by Father Baker: a refuge for unmarried mothers, with the same sympathy and charity that he always manifested, care of the infants and small children, and adoption services.

Our Lady of Victory Hospital has been expanded to meet the needs of the community, with two additional wings constructed — just as the Infant Home has been renovated, and improvements made in other buildings to maintain their efficiency and to improve the assistance given to those entrusted to their care.

One constant link with the early days has been the Sisters of St. Joseph, who were at the homes before Father Baker came, and whose valiant assistance he treasured throughout his lifetime, as Monsignor McPherson does now.

After Our Lady of Victory's assistance, we may be sure that Father Baker valued highly the help of the many Sisters

143

of St. Joseph who labored so hard and so tirelessly for the little ones, the sick, the hungry, the homeless children who came there for help.

Another link with the past, which has been maintained constantly since established by Father Baker, is *The Victorian* magazine, now as then distributed nationally as a well-known Catholic family magazine. Interestingly — to show how the thread of Father Baker's influence continues — *The Victorian* is now edited by Monsignor Nelson W. Logal, whose parents named him after Father Baker.

The care of boys was the first work assigned to Father Baker when he came to Limestone Hill in 1876; naturally, it is still a major activity of Our Lady of Victory Homes of Charity. With the change in the needs of the boys, however, a new approach has begun, with particular attention being paid to the needs of teen-age boys.

This is being done through Baker Hall, named for Father Baker. Three foster homes have been purchased and others are being built as they become needed to care for these teen-agers. The boys come to Baker Hall to live for a while, and then may be transferred to Nelson House or McPherson House, foster homes in residential areas which offer a family type of living. These are family-type dwellings, no different from others in the area, where the boys and their house "mother and father" work, pray, and play together as a Catholic-family unit. Baker Hall has a threefold program: the group approach, individual guidance, and foster care.

Another strong link with the past is the means by which Our Lady of Victory Homes are financed. In the early days, Father Baker would sit down at his rolltop desk and write letters by hand to Catholic women throughout the country, asking their assistance for this work of Our Lady of Victory. Nowadays it is not necessary to go through the same laborious process — but now, as then, the support for this work of Our Lady of Victory Homes of Charity comes from donors throughout the country. Many are still alive who knew Father Baker and his work; others are the children of those who heard from their parents of this charitable enterprise; and still others are new clients of Our Lady of Victory, who remember the work through their offerings, and through bequests.

The past and the present are closely linked in these works of charity — works which are a tremendous monument to Our Lady of Victory, and to her clients who have helped erect it, not the least of which was Monsignor Nelson H. Baker.

INDEX

147

148